# Piping on Cakes

Christine Flinn

SEARCH PRESS

First published 2016

Search Press Limited
Wellwood, North Farm Road,
Tunbridge Wells, Kent TN2 3DR

Text copyright © Christine Flinn 2016

Photographs by Paul Bricknell at Search Press Studios

Photographs and design copyright © Search Press Ltd 2016

ISBN: 978-1-78221-237-9

**Suppliers**

If you have difficulty in obtaining any of the materials and equipment mentioned in this book, then please visit the Search Press website for details of suppliers:
www.searchpress.com

**Publisher's note**

All the step-by-step photographs in this book feature the author, Christine Flinn, demonstrating piping on cakes. No models have been used.

Printed in China

## Dedication

This book is dedicated to my parents, Colin and Rosemary Burt, my husband, Chris and daughters, Amy, Rachel and Lisa.

## Acknowledgements

With thanks to Annie Ralph for the music score on page 39, Paul Bricknell for the amazing photographs, and Sophie Kersey for sorting out the overspill of text.

# CONTENTS

# INTRODUCTION

When I was a child, I had amazing birthday cakes, created by my cousin, Margaret. I decided very early on that when I was old enough, I wanted to learn how to decorate cakes just like her.

The first cake decoration class I attended was a basic evening class at the local high school. Yearning for more formal training, I enrolled in a City and Guilds Course in cake decoration and flour confectionery at the College of Art and Technology, Newcastle upon Tyne. Nowadays, I earn my living by teaching cake decoration both at home and abroad, demonstrating various cake decorating techniques and writing sugarcraft articles.

Cake decorating has changed a lot since I attended my first class in the late 1970s. At that time, celebration cakes were royal-iced fruit cakes, with the main form of decoration being run-outs and piped linework. Fondant (sugarpaste) was only used for slab cakes which were sold by the slice. This had all changed by the millennium, when most celebration cakes were covered with fondant (sugarpaste) and the cake of choice became sponge.

It should be remembered that no design is completely new – they are always influenced by what has come before, as well as by what is current in popular culture and the designer's own sources of inspiration. Stacked cakes were considered ultra-modern in the 1990s, yet if one took the time to glance at cake decorating books of the late 1800s, this would be completely contradicted. The stacked cake design of the 1800s fell out of favour and was replaced with what our generation would consider the more traditional pillared tiered cakes.

In recent years, piped designs on celebration cakes have started to come back into fashion. I hope the instructions and designs within this book will inspire you to pick up a piping bag and have a go – it really is easy, provided you follow the golden rules on page 34! For the greatest sense of achievement, try and design your own cake using the techniques shown in this book.

Most of the designs are suitable for a cake covered in fondant (sugarpaste) or a cake coated with royal icing, but to achieve a similar effect as the Indian Inlaid Cake on page 72 on a royal-iced cake, the inlaid shapes would need to be made as run-outs using a No. 0 nozzle and then attached to the surface cake with a few dots of royal icing before commencing the overpiping.

For a balanced look, a round cake is best divided into three, six, nine, or twelve sections, and a square cake into two, four, eight or twelve. Most of the designs in this book have been created on small cakes: 15cm (6in) to 20.3cm (8in), but if you wish to use a larger cake, the easiest option will be to create more sections (for example three sections would become six).

I have shown you how to create your own paper templates to fit your cake, but design templates are supplied at the back of the book. Templates are also provided so that you can practise piping the basic shapes.

A right-handed person should find it easier to pipe from left to right, but if you are left-handed, remember to mirror image all the designs and pipe from right to left.

# CAKES

All the designs in this book are feasible on a sponge cake, but the density and shelf life of this type of cake means it's not advisable to coat it with royal icing, so cover it with fondant (sugarpaste) instead. The basketweave on the Rose Basket (page 46) could be piped with buttercream if using a sponge cake.

## Fruit cake recipe

|  | Round/heart | Square | Oval |
|---|---|---|---|
|  | 20cm (8in) | 20cm (8in) | 20 x 15cm (8 x 6in) |
| Butter (block) | 300g (10oz) | 420g (14oz) | 240g (8oz) |
| Soft brown sugar | 300g (10oz) | 420g (14oz) | 240g (8oz) |
| Eggs | 300g (10oz) | 420g (14oz) | 240g (8oz) |
| Plain flour (all-purpose) | 300g (10oz) | 420g (14oz) | 240g (8oz) |
| Salt | pinch | pinch | pinch |
| Mixed spices | 6.25ml (1¼tsp) | 8.75ml (1¾tsp) | 5ml (1tsp) |
| Ground nutmeg | 1.88ml (³⁄₈tsp) | 4.38ml (⁷⁄₈tsp) | 2.5ml (½tsp) |
| Mixed candied peel (chopped) | 150g (5oz) | 210g (7oz) | 120g (4oz) |
| Glacé cherries (chopped) | 150g (5oz) | 210g (7oz) | 120g (4oz) |
| Raisins | 150g (5oz) | 210g (7oz) | 120g (4oz) |
| Sultanas | 300g (10oz) | 420g (14oz) | 420g (8oz) |
| Currants | 450g (15oz) | 630g (21oz) | 360g (12oz) |

## Notes

- The weight of egg is without the shell.
- A 17.5cm (7in) square cake requires the same amount of cake mixture as a 20cm (8in) round cake. Likewise a 22.5cm (9in) round cake requires the same amount of mixture as a 20cm (8in) square cake; and a 20 x 15cm (8 x 6in) oval cake requires the same amount as a 17.5cm (7in) round or 15cm (6in) square cake.

# Lining a cake tin

When creating a celebration cake, it is essential that you have a good foundation to work on: a cake with smooth, straight sides. This is why it is important to line a cake tin correctly.

## Square

**1** Take a strip of baking parchment 25cm (10in) in depth and fold it in half. Create a single fold 5cm (2in) from one end.

**2** Place the strip inside the cake tin, line the fold up with one corner, then firmly fold the strip at each corner.

**3** Remove the strip from the cake tin. Fold the base edge up by approx. 2.5cm (1in).

**4** Open up this fold and re-fold the strip at the corners. Cut a large 'V' shape of 45 degrees up to the base fold, at the point of each corner fold (see the photograph below).

**5** Place the strip of baking parchment in the cake tin. Cut a further two pieces of baking parchment to fit the base of the cake tin.

## Round

**1** Take a strip of baking parchment 25cm (10in) in depth and fold it in half.

**2** Wrap the strip around the cake tin, leaving a 5cm (2in) overlap, and cut off the surplus.

**3** Fold up the base edge by approx 2.5cm (1in).

**4** Open up this fold and snip all along the base section at 45 degrees (see the photograph).

**5** Place the strip of baking parchment in the cake tin.

**6** Cut two discs of baking parchment a fraction smaller than the base of the cake tin and place in the tin.

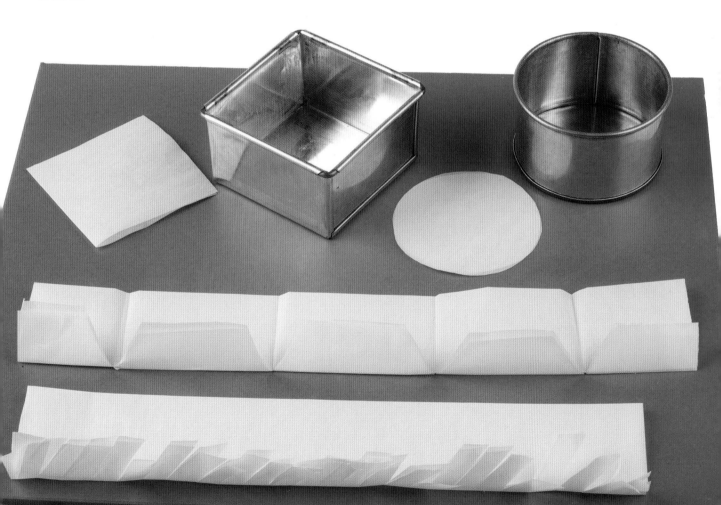

## Method

**1** Pre-heat the oven to gas mark 2, 300°F, 150°C, 110°C fan assisted.

**2** Double line the cake tin base and sides with baking parchment (see previous page).

**3** Cream the butter and soft brown sugar together.

**4** In a separate bowl, combine all the dry ingredients in the order shown (see page 8), stirring between each addition to ensure that all the dried fruit is coated in the flour mixture.

**5** Lightly whip the eggs in a jug.

**6** Pour a small amount of egg into the creamed butter/sugar mixture. Stir in using your bare hand.

**7** Add a small amount of the dry mix to the sugar mixture and stir, using your bare hand.

**8** Repeat step 6 and 7 until all the ingredients are combined.

**9** Transfer the cake batter to the prepared cake tin (see previous page).

**10** Use a spatula to smooth and level the mixture in the tin.

**11** Wet your hand with cold water and lightly rub your palm over the surface to leave a film of water on top of the cake batter.

**12** Wrap the outside of the tin with a double layer of brown paper (secured with a piece of string) and transfer to the pre-heated oven. Alternatively, use the covered tin method (see below), especially if you have a fan assisted oven, as these tend to blast heat at the cake. Place your filled cake tin on a baking sheet (the baking sheet needs to be no smaller than the size of the covering tin). Invert a cake tin at least 5cm (2in) larger than the filled cake tin, to cover it. This must create a sealed unit (it should not be possible to see the filled cake tin). Using this method stops the cake sides from becoming too dark and crisp, and it also creates a flat cake with no dome.

### *The covered tin method*

## Cake baking and feeding tips

• As a rough guide (each oven is different), the cooking time is approx. thirty minutes for every 2.5cm (1in) of the tin, i.e. 20cm (8in) would be approx. four hours. If you cannot smell the cake, it is nowhere near baked, so do not open the oven door.

• If the surface of the cake has cracked during baking, this suggests that the oven is too hot, as the outside has crusted over before the internal structure has finished expanding. Reduce the oven temperature next time you bake this fruit cake.

• Once baked, the cake must be allowed to go cold in the tin overnight or for twelve hours. This allows the cake to settle. If you empty it onto a cooling rack too soon, then you might end up with a cake with sloping sides.

• Decant the fruit cake from the cake tin and place on a cooling rack. Remove all of the baking parchment. Turn it the right way up.

Feed the cake with brandy – for a small cake, pour 15ml (1 tablespoon) of brandy in a slow spiralling stream on top of the cold fruit cake. Leave for an hour.

• Wrap the fruit cake in a fresh sheet of baking parchment to protect it from dust and insects, and store in a cool, dry environment. There is no need to wrap the cake in aluminium foil or cling film or store in an airtight container. It must be allowed to breathe as it matures.

• Feed the cake with brandy once a month, alternating between the top and bottom.

# ROYAL ICING

There are three egg options when making royal icing: fresh egg white, pure dried albumen and fortified dried albumen (Meri-white). Their attributes are described on page 14. Glycerine is added to royal icing which is to be used for coating a cake, to prevent it becoming too hard. It should only be added to royal icing once it is at full peak (see step 4 in the method, opposite). The normal ratio is 5ml (1tsp) glycerine for every 454g (1lb) of icing sugar (powdered sugar) used. Royal icing for run-outs, lace pieces or extension work should not contain glycerine, as it needs to dry rock solid. For regular piping, it does not matter whether or not the royal icing includes glycerine.

When coating a cake with royal icing, always try and make up enough for three coats. 454g (1lb) of royal icing is sufficient for three coats on a 15cm (6in) cake.

When you start working with royal icing, it is best to make it by hand, not in a mixer, so that you feel the texture change. Most hand-held mixers beat too fast for making royal icing. If you do use a mixer, it should be a bench-top mixer, and make the icing on the slowest speed available.

All the equipment used to make royal icing must be grease free, as even a tiny smear will create heavy, unusable royal icing. If you can't keep a dedicated set of equipment just for royal icing, scour your equipment with a salt/water paste before use.

## Royal icing recipe options:

| 15ml (1tbsp) Meri-white | *or* | 118ml (½ cup) CK meringue powder |
| 60ml (4tbsp) cold water | | 235ml (1 cup) cold water |
| Approx. 454g (1lb) icing sugar (powdered sugar), sifted | | Approx. 1.25 kg (2lb 12oz) to 1.36kg (3lb) icing sugar (powdered sugar), sifted |

**Glycerine**

If using glycerine, add 5ml (1tsp) glycerine for every 454g (1lb) of icing sugar (powdered sugar) used.

**Sugar**

The reason why the sugar amount is just an approximation is the fact that water has a skin, so you can have a convex or a concave tablespoon of water.

## Small quantity of royal icing:

5ml (1tsp) Meri-white
20ml (4tsp) cold water
Approx. 150g (5oz) icing sugar (powdered sugar), sifted

If using fresh egg whites, put them in a bowl, cover with a clean cloth or kitchen paper and leave for several hours before using, to allow some of the water to evaporate, making a stronger royal icing. Fresh egg white or reconstituted dried albumen should be in a 1:6 ratio with the sugar, so weigh the egg white and then multiply by six to find the weight of icing sugar (powdered sugar) required.

## Method

**1** Stir or mix the Meri-white (or CK meringue powder) in the water until no powder lumps are visible and the liquid has a slight froth.

**2** Add approx. one-third of the icing sugar (powdered sugar) and mix until it is all incorporated – it should be slightly translucent.

**3** Add half of the remaining sugar to the mixture and mix until it is all incorporated (don't forget to scrape down the sides of the bowl). The icing will no longer be translucent.

**4** Add most of the remaining icing sugar (powdered sugar) and continue to mix until the mixture is at full peak: when the spatula is removed from the bowl, the take-off point of the icing should stand to attention, without flopping. The icing should have a nice satin sheen; it should not look wet. If the icing will not come to a peak, add the remaining icing sugar (powdered sugar) and continue mixing.

**5** If the royal icing is being used for coating a cake, fold in 5ml (1 teaspoon) of glycerine for every 454g (1lb) of icing sugar used.

### Trouble-shooting and tips:

If you are new to royal icing, use these tips to help you get the mixture right.

- Problem: the equipment has a smear of grease on it, resulting in a heavy mass of dull icing. Discard and start again.
- Problem: you stopped mixing as soon as all the sugar was incorporated. You need to mix for longer.
- Problem: you added too much icing sugar (powdered sugar).
- Dark colours can cause problems – the quantity of food colour added could upset the balance of the mixture. For this reason, use good quality, strong food colours such as droplets; not paste food colours. For black, red or navy blue, I recommend pure powder food colours that you reconstitute in water before use.
- Royal icing is at its strongest on the day it is made (the older the icing, the weaker it becomes). If it has been sitting for more than a couple of hours, it must always be re-beaten by hand to bring it back up to peak before using.
- Try not to use an icing sugar (powdered sugar) with more than 1.5% anti-caking agent, as the royal icing will be short, brittle and unusable.
- Pre-mixes are normally usable, but can be expensive. The whole packet needs to be made up in one go, as if you use just a few spoonfuls, you might not get the right proportion of albumen to sugar.
- Royal icing has a usable shelf life of seven days. The older it is, the less is can be used for.
- It should always be stored at room temperature and not in the fridge.
- The bowl of royal icing should always be covered with a damp cloth.
- It's not a good idea to store royal icing in plastic containers. Glass or ceramic are best, as plastic can harbour grease in the score marks caused by previous use.

13

# MATERIALS

## Cake covering

**Royal icing** is a traditional icing used for coating a cake, as well as creating the decoration on iced cakes. This icing acquired the name 'royal' when it was used on Queen Victoria's wedding cake in 1840. Before this it was known as 'snow icing'.

**Fondant** (**sugarpaste**) is a sugar dough that can be rolled out to decorate cakes. It was first mentioned in the 1600s in Manchester, UK. It is known by various names: fondant in the USA, sugarpaste in the UK and RTF (ready to roll fondant) or plastic icing in Australia.

**Marzipan**, or **almond paste**, is made from ground almonds and sugar, and is used to create a barrier between a fruit cake and its coating of icing. Home-made almond paste was traditionally bound together with egg yolks, but this is now classed as a food risk since the paste is uncooked, so use liquid glucose instead.

Fondant and marzipan can be coloured with **paste food colours** (not shown).

**Vodka** Used to sterilise the surface of marzipan, as well as creating a sticky surface to secure fondant (sugarpaste). Any clear drinking alcohol, such as gin or white rum, is suitable.

**Raspberry jam (jelly)** is used as a filling for sponge cakes. The tartness of the raspberry helps balance the sweetness of the cake.

**Buttercream** Used as a filling, as well as a masking to secure the fondant (sugarpaste) to a sponge cake.

**Apricot glaze** Used as a masking for fruit cakes. It must be always brought to the boil before use. Apricot is the best choice due to its neutral flavour and colour. It also has a high pectin content, so is less likely to go mouldy.

**Icing sugar (powdered sugar)** Used as a dusting on the work surfaces for rolling out marzipan and fondant (sugarpaste). Also used when creating buttercream and royal icing. For best quality, the anti-caking agent (often cornflour/maize starch) should be no more than 1.5%.

**Glycerine** This is added to royal icing when used for coating, to stop it fully drying out, so the cake can be cut with a knife and does not a need a hammer and chisel!

**Royal icing packet mix** Various brands are available if you prefer not to make the royal icing from scratch. However, remember that you need to make up the whole box, rather than just a couple of spoonfuls, to be sure of achieving the correct proportion of albumen to sugar.

**Dried albumen (egg white)** For making royal icing. It needs to be reconstituted with water and allowed to stand for several hours before use. It is advisable to pass the liquid through a fine mesh (knee high or pop sock) before use, to remove any undissolved particles.

**Fortified dried albumen (Meri-white)** This powder contains dried albumen as well as brightener and stabiliser, so it creates a whiter royal icing than fresh egg whites or pure dried albumen. It is ready for use as soon as the powder is dissolved in water (unlike pure dried albumen, which requires a standing time). Be warned that it often contains wheat starch.

**Fresh egg white** Used to create royal icing. If time permits, cover with a clean cloth and leave for several hours before use. This allows some of the water to evaporate and thus makes a stronger royal icing.

**Edger** (black)  A smoother at a 90 degree angle, to help create straight sides.

**Smoother** (rounded on four edges)  Used to smooth rolled out fondant (sugarpaste).

**Rolling pin**  This must be large enough for the job: it needs to be no less than 5cm (2in) larger than the width of the cake plus twice the depth of the cake. So for a 15cm (6in) cake of 7.5cm (3in) depth, you need a rolling pin no less than 35cm (14in) long.

**Space bars**  Used to create an even thickness to rolled out marzipan or fondant (sugarpaste).

**Palette knife**  Used to fill or mask a cake, or coat it with royal icing.

**Metal side scraper**  Used for smoothing the sides of a royal-iced cake. It needs to be at least 2.5cm (1in) taller than the depth of the cake.

**Plastic side scraper**  Used to smooth the sides of the cake if you do not have an edger.

**Straight edge**  Used to create a smooth surface on the top of a royal-iced cake.

**Ham knife**  Used to level a cake as well as to create a smooth surface on the top of a royal-iced cake.

*Clockwise from top left: vodka, raspberry jam, buttercream, apricot glaze, icing sugar (powdered sugar), glycerine, royal icing packet mix, packet of dried albumen, tub of fortified dried albumen (Meri-white), fresh egg white (in glass), white fondant (sugarpaste), marzipan, black edger, white smoother, rolling pin, space bars, palette knife, metal and plastic side scrapers, ham knife, straight edge.*

# Piping tools

The best piping nozzles are seamless. These are not cheap, but if looked after, they will last a lifetime. Piping nozzles should always be washed by hand using a nozzle brush; never place them in a dishwasher. The tips are very delicate, so the nozzles should be stored in a box fitted with dividers so they will not rattle around. On no account should a pin or anything similar be inserted into the tip of the nozzle, as this will damage it and it will never pipe a true straight line again. Seamed nozzles can cause various problems including a piped line that curls or twists. Shown below, clockwise from top left are:

**Piping bag holder**  Keeps the tip of the piping nozzle damp, as well as keeping the piping bags in order.

**Parchment piping bags**  Four sizes are shown, to go with to the size of the piping nozzles.

**Edible liquid food colours** (droplets)  These blend into any form of icing which is suitable for a piping bag.

**Pipettes and shot glass**  Ideal for reconstituting pure powder food colour before adding to royal icing.

**Pure powder food colour**  These are not petal dust. They are ideal when strong colours are required in royal icing.

**Baking parchment** (cut into triangles)  Various sizes for creating piping bags.

**Plastic side scraper**  Used as a surface on which to paddle small quantities of royal icing.

**Disposable plastic piping bags**  The 30cm (12in) size is used with the piping nozzle adapter and the grass nozzle.

**Piping nozzle adapter** and **grass nozzle**

**Knee highs (pop socks)** – used to sieve small quantities of royal icing when using fine or ultrafine piping nozzles (1, 0, or 00).

**Nozzle brush**  Designed to clean a piping nozzle without damaging it.

**Paper scissors**  Paper blunts scissors, so keep a pair of scissors just for that purpose.

**Fine sable paintbrushes**  Natural bristle brushes which are soft but firm. They can be reshaped from a point to a flat tip and then back again.

**Palette knives** in 10cm (4in) and 20cm (8in).

**Piping nozzles** and subdivided **nozzle box** – it is vital to look after piping nozzles.

**Tip**

If the tip of a nozzle is damaged or partially blocked, when you are trying to pipe with it, the piped line will curl back on itself.

# Other tools and materials

A lot of equipment is not essential, however it makes decorating a cake a lot easier if you have it to hand. Shown on the right are a food dehydrator for drying run-outs from run sugar work, and a bench-top mixer for mixing cakes and royal icing.

Shown below are my homemade cake tilter (two pieces of wood joined with hinges and a wooden dowel with non-slip matting. All lines need to be piped with the help of gravity, (not against it) and this simple, cheap design does the job. The flexible smoother is for smoothing royal icing on a curved surface such as a chamfered cake drum. You need an anglepoise lamp to dry the surface of run sugar items quickly, retaining a high gloss. A sieve is used to sift icing sugar (powdered sugar). Place cakes on a turntable for coating with royal icing; this one is 12.5cm (5in) high. A turntable should have a smooth turning action. The flat turntable is ideal when piping a design on the top of a cake. The tilting turntable (Handcock) needs to be heavy so it does not tip over when heavy cakes are placed at a steep angle; it needs brackets to hold the cake drum in place and, most importantly, it must have total flexibility in the angle of tilt.

Keep dedicated glass bowls and a spatula for royal icing, as a tiny smear of grease can ruin a batch. Good quality cake tins are essential. Round, square, heart-shaped, hexagonal and oval ones are used in this book. They should have good shape, depth and weight.

Various shaped cake drums, 13mm (½in) deep are needed. A cake drum needs to be able to hold the weight of the cake without bending. Satin ribbons are used to edge the cake drums, attached with non-toxic glue stick.

Baking parchment is used for lining tins. Wax paper is traditionally used for creating run-outs on but food-grade acetate (butcher's wrap) is easier to use as you can see the design through it and it is not so sensitive to temperature. It is also used for piped flowers.

A scriber is used to mark a design onto a cake. A veining/Dresden tool is used to texture fondant (sugarpaste). Tweezers are ideal for holding and positioning stamen cottons, used for the antennae on piped butterflies. An artist's palette knife has various uses including releasing run-outs. Keep dedicated scissors for cutting paper and ribbons.

Sheets of perspex (plexiglass) are used for embossed designs, as well as run-outs. A set square ensures straight lines in designs, while a ruler is used for measurements. Masking tape holds templates in place.

Food-grade acetate (butcher's wrap) is used to create run-outs on. A small piece of sponge foam is used to texture royal icing. White vegetable fat acts as a releasing agent for run-outs. Digital weighing scales are used for weighing ingredients. A roll of cash register receipt paper is useful for creating templates for the sides of cakes.

Edible spray varnish is used to seal and create a shine on run-outs after they have been sprayed with the metallic gold and bronze spray. Edible liquid metallic paint is used on the piped chain on the Steampunk cake. Cocktail sticks or toothpicks are used for piping roses. Double-sided sticky tape is used to create a flat bow. A puffer is used to remove any loose particles from the surface of a cake, since blowing on cakes is classed as spitting.

# TECHNIQUES

## Cake covering

Covering a fruit cake with
marzipan ready for a flat
coating of royal icing

In the past, the weight of marzipan was
the same as the cake it covered, with
two-thirds of this used to cover the top,
but these days a 5mm (¼in) thickness
on the top and sides is standard.
To achieve a nicely coated royal-iced
cake, it's important that the foundation
cake is level and smooth, so do not
rush this stage.

### Tips for preparing the cake and marzipan

• A cake should never be turned upside down to decorate it, as the cake
crumb (grain) will be going the wrong way and it is more likely to crumble
when cut. Level the top of the cake instead.

• Bring the apricot glaze to the boil and use a knife to apply a thin layer
to the top of the cake only. Using a pastry brush for this purpose is not
recommended as there is a risk of leaving bristles on the cake surface.

• Knead the marzipan on a clean, dry work surface, not on icing sugar
(powdered sugar). Do not roll the marzipan out on the same area that it has
been kneaded on, as there will be a residue on the work surface, which will
cause the marzipan to stick.

• Space bars should always be used to create an even thickness of
marzipan. However, it is important that the marzipan is rolled until it stops
growing in size, and not until you think it is big enough to cover the cake.

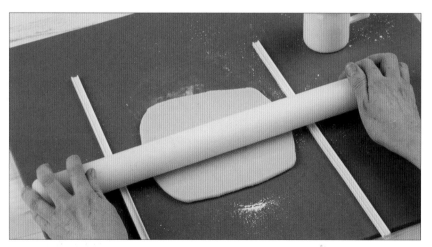

1 Lightly dust the rolling-out surface with icing sugar (powdered sugar). Do
not use cornflour/cornstach as it will cause the marzipan to ferment. Place
the space bars either side of the marzipan. Roll it out, turning it 45 degrees
frequently for a round cake and 90 degrees for a square. Do not turn the
marzipan over.

2 Coat the top of the cake with a
mask (thin layer) of hot apricot
glaze. Re-dust the rolling out surface
and flip the marzipan over. Invert the
cake (apricot glaze side down) and
place on the marzipan. Press the
cake down firmly.

3 Trim the marzipan level with
the sides of the cake using
a palette knife. Take hold of the
cake, flip it the right way up and
place it on the cake drum.

4 Using a knife, apply a thin layer of the hot apricot glaze to the cake sides. Roll a piece of marzipan into a sausage and follow previous instructions for rolling out. Cut one of the long edges straight and mitre one of the short edges (see inset). Attach to the cake side with the mitred edge protruding by 5mm (¼in). Use an edger to smooth the marzipan onto the cake side.

5 Mitre the other end of the strip of marzipan.

6 Roll out another piece of marzipan into a sausage and repeat the above, butting up the mitred ends. Repeat for the remaining sides.

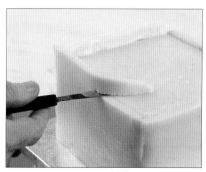

7 Trim the marzipan level with the top of the cake. A royal-iced cake is all about sharp edges, so make sure you hold the knife level with the cake top and not at an angle. Leave the marzipaned cake for twenty-four hours to skin over before coating with royal icing.

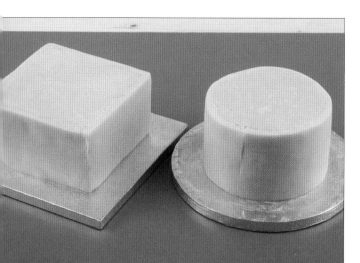

*A round cake is covered in a similar way, except that the marzipan for the top should be turned by approx. 45 degrees each time while rolling it out, to help keep it in a circular shape. Only one long strip of marzipan is required for the side. Cut one of the long edges to neaten it, roll the strip of marzipan up and then unwind it around the cake, with the cut edge at the base. Overlap the marzipan where it meets and cut through both layers to make a neat join. Remove the surplus marzipan. Use an edger or a plastic side scraper to smooth the cake sides with a backwards and forwards motion.*

# Covering a round cake with marzipan ready for fondant (sugarpaste)

It is not essential to apply a layer of marzipan to a sponge cake before covering with fondant (sugarpaste), but it will help you to achieve a better quality finish. Fruit cakes do need to be covered with marzipan. Apply the apricot glaze and knead and roll out the marzipan as on page 18, but turning 45 degrees with each turn to achieve a circular shape.

1 Lift the marzipan up using the rolling pin. Make sure that the surface that was touching the work surface is the side that touches the cake. Cover the cake. Lift the rolling pin as it comes to the cake edge closest to you, allowing the marzipan to drop onto the cake side (if you use a downward action, you will dent the top corner edge of the cake).

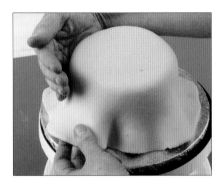

2 Gently smooth the top of the cake with the palm of your hand. Smooth the marzipan onto to the side of the cake using your right hand, turning the cake on the turntable as you work. Use your left hand to stop the marzipan going into folds. Trim the marzipan 13mm (½in) away from the cake.

3 Use a side scraper to gently push the cut edge of the marzipan towards the cake until a crease line is visible.

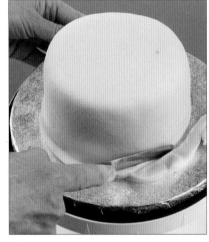

4 Carefully cut the marzipan along the crease line.

5 Polish and smooth the side of the cake using an edger with a backwards and forwards motion.

6 Smooth the top of the cake using the smoother with a circular motion. Finish smoothing using the dip in the base of your palm along the top corner edge of the cake, with a backwards and forwards motion. Check the top edge of the cake and fill in any indentations with a small piece of marzipan. Ideally leave the marzipan to skin over before covering with fondant (sugarpaste).

# Covering a square cake with marzipan ready for fondant (sugarpaste)

Prepare the cake and roll out the marzipan as for the round cake, and cover the cake. Gently smooth the marzipan on the top of the cake with the palm of your hand. If you feel an air pocket, carefully lift the marzipan up from the side of the cake and stroke the air out.

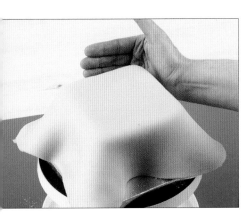

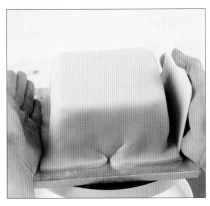

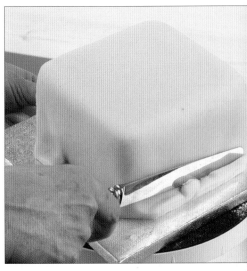

1 Carefully smooth the marzipan onto to the side of the cake, concentrating on the corners first: cup your hand and press the marzipan into the corner using an upward stroke. Use your left hand to stop the marzipan going into folds.

2 Trim the marzipan 13mm (½in) away from the cake. Use a side scraper to gently push the cut edge of the marzipan towards the cake until a crease line is visible.

3 Carefully cut the marzipan across the corners, then along the crease line.

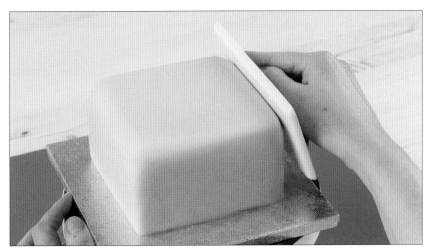

4 Polish and smooth the side of the cake using an edger with a backwards and forwards motion.

5 Polish and smooth the top and side of the cake using the smoother, moving from the side over the top edge and into the middle. Polish and smooth the corner edges using the palm of your hand. Check that the top edge of the cake is smooth and fill in any indentations with small pieces of marzipan. Ideally, leave the marzipan to skin over before covering with fondant (sugarpaste).

# Coating a square cake with royal icing

A sponge cake is not suitable to be coated in royal icing, because of the density of the structure and shelf life. It is standard practice to apply three coats of royal icing to all celebration cakes, though up to seven may be used for competition pieces for an ultra-smooth finish.

**Tip**

There are two choices of tool for levelling the icing on top: firstly a ham knife held firmly in one hand with three fingers placed centrally on the flat side of the blade. Pressure is applied with the fingers to create a smooth coat. Alternatively, use a straight edge balanced on two fingers of each hand, with thumbs on top to apply pressure.

1 Apply a small amount of royal icing to the top of the cake with the large palette knife. Ensure the tip of the knife runs centrally down the top of the cake and paddle the royal icing.

2 Turn the cake 90 degrees on the turntable and repeat the paddling. Continue to add royal icing and paddle it on the surface of the cake until it reaches the edge of the cake.

3 Remove the cake from the turntable and place on a non-slip mat. Working from the centre of the cake with ever increasing lengths of stroke, paddle the royal icing on the cake using the straight edge or knife. Do not turn the straight edge or knife over – the icing should be on the underside only.

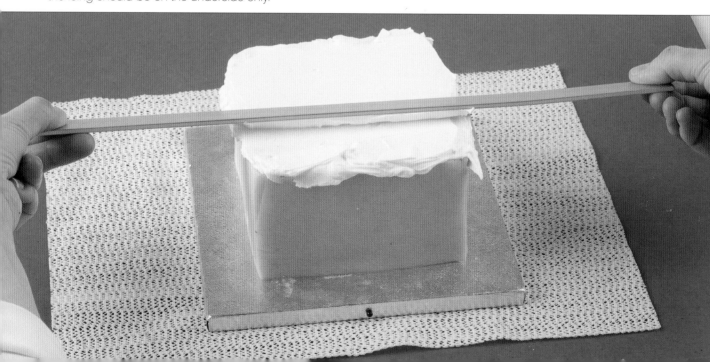

**4** Once the paddle stroke is long enough to go from the top to the bottom of the cake, take the straight edge down and off the bottom edge in one quick movement.

**Tip**

Place a piece of masking tape (or a pin) on the side of the cake board at the take-off point of the straight edge. This ensures that the take-off point is different on the cake each time you add a coat of royal icing. The take-off points should be at 6, 9 and 12 o'clock.

**5** Remove the surplus royal icing from the top edge of the cake with small downward strokes of the palette knife, with the blade vertical rather than at an angle. Wipe the blade clean with each action using a clean, damp cloth. Unless you are making cakes commercially, I recommend that you leave the top of the cake to dry for eight hours, before applying royal icing to the sides.

**Tip**

On no account should you use a sweeping action with the palette knife around the top edge of the cake to remove the surplus royal icing. This will create an uneven surface which will cause problems when applying the next coat.

6 Apply a little royal icing to the side of the cake where you have marked the board (see the pin). Keep the tip of the palette knife touching the board as you paddle the royal icing on to the side. Slope the knife to work the royal icing up to the top edge or down to the base of the cake. Continue until the whole side is covered, applying extra royal icing if necessary. Remove the cake from the turntable and place on the non-slip mat.

7 Hold the metal side scraper firmly, with your fingers evenly spaced. The base of the scraper should always touch the cake board. Hold the scraper slightly in advance of the corner edge of the cake side and slowly, in a single, smooth action, move it along the side, then pull it towards you, off the cake. If you stop, you will create a line or ridge. Note that it is normal on a first coat for the marzipan to show through the royal icing in places.

**Side scraping tips**

• Make sure you apply even pressure with every finger – if you don't apply enough with your little finger, you will end up with sloping sides, otherwise known as the 'lighthouse effect'.

• If the angle of the side scraper to the surface of the cake is too acute, a smooth surface will not be achieved. If the angle is too obtuse, you will end up removing all the royal icing from the side of the cake.

8 Remove the surplus royal icing from the top edge of the cake. Use small cutting actions with the palette knife blade pointing towards the centre of the cake, level with the top of the cake and not at an angle. Wipe clean with a damp, clean cloth with each action. Do not use a sweeping action along the edge of the cake, or this will leave a lip, causing problems for subsequent coats.

9 Remove the surplus royal icing from the side of the cake using a cutting action (the knife should be moved towards the centre of the cake side). Wipe clean any royal icing which is visible on the cake drum – do not allow it to dry. Leave the coated cake sides to dry (ideally for no less than four hours) before coating the other two sides.

### Subsequent coats

The second coat is exactly the same as the first, apart from the fact the marked side on the edge of the cake drum needs to be at 9 o'clock when removing the surplus royal icing from the top with the straight edge or knife. Leave this coat to dry (ideally no less than eight hours) before coating the sides. The third coat is the same as the second except that the marked edge of the cake drum needs to be at 12 o'clock when smoothing the top.

# Coating a cake drum with royal icing

A coated cake drum always creates a more professional look to the finished celebration cake.

## A square cake drum

1 Apply a small amount of royal icing (normal consistency) to the cake drum, and paddle it with the palette knife, adding more until it is completely covered.

2 Hold the edge of a metal side scraper level with the cake drum and, in one smooth action, pull it along the cake drum. Turn the cake on the turntable and repeat the action on the remaining sides. For a chamfered cake drum, use a flexi-scraper.

3 Use small, downward cutting actions with the palette knife to remove the surplus royal icing at the edges of the cake drum. Wipe the blade with a clean, damp cloth on each action. Clean the edge of the cake drum with the clean, damp cloth. Leave the royal icing to dry for no less than four hours before continuing.

4 Place a small amount of royal icing in a glass jug or bowl. Add a little water to create a thick run sugar consistency. Cover the bowl with a damp cloth and leave to stand for no less than fifteen minutes before continuing. Cut through the air pockets (bubbles) on the surface of the royal icing with a knife.

5 Cover the turntable with a piece of plastic food wrap. Apply the run sugar to the coated cake drum and continue applying more it until it is completely covered.

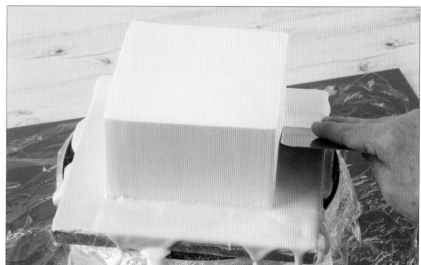

6 Hold the edge of a metal side scraper level with the cake drum and in one smooth action, pull the scraper along the cake drum. Turn the cake on the turntable and repeat the action on the remaining sides. For a chamfered cake drum, use a flexi-scraper.

7 Clean up the side edge of the cake drum using a palette knife and a clean, damp cloth. Leave the run-sugar coated cake drum to dry completely (twenty-four hours) before commencing the piped decoration.

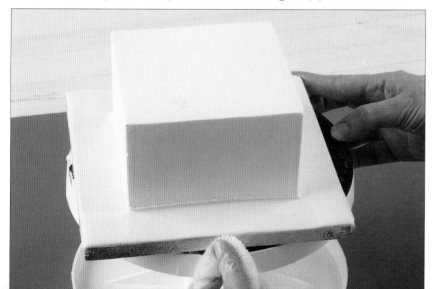

### Covering a round cake drum

This is the same as a square cake drum, but the levelling with the metal side scraper needs to be done in one smooth action – so hold the turntable edge and turn it the same way as you would for smoothing the coating at the sides of a round cake.

# Coating a round cake with royal icing

1 Apply a small amount of royal icing to the top of the cake with a palette knife. Keep the tip of the knife in the centre of the cake and paddle the royal icing while turning the cake on the turntable. Continue until the icing reaches the edge of the cake, applying more to the centre of the cake top if necessary as you go.

2 Remove the cake from the turntable and place on a non-slip mat. Working from the centre of the cake with every increasing lengths of stroke, paddle the royal icing on the cake using the ham knife. Do not turn the knife over – the icing should be on the underside only.

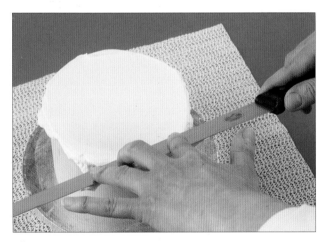

3 Once the paddle stroke is long enough to go from the top to the bottom of the cake, take the knife straight down and off the bottom edge of the cake in one smooth action. Mark the cake drum with masking tape or a pin to remind you of the take-off point.

**Tip**

On no account should you use a sweeping action with the palette knife around the top edge of the cake to remove the surplus royal icing – as this will create a ridge or uneven surface which will cause problems when applying the next coat.

4 Remove the surplus royal icing from the top edge of the cake with small downward strokes of the palette knife, with the blade vertical. Wipe the blade clean with each action using a clean, damp cloth.

5 The completed top coat. The pin marks the take-off point of the knife when smoothing the top for this first coat, to ensure that the take-off point is different for each subsequent coat. Unless you are working in a trade environment, I highly recommend that you leave the royal icing on the top of the cake at least eight hours to dry, before applying a coat to the side.

6 Apply a small amount of royal icing to the side of the cake. Keep the tip of the knife touching the cake drum at all times and paddle the royal icing while turning the cake on the turntable. Slope the angle of the palette knife to work the icing up to the top edge or down to the base of the cake.

7 Continue to paddle the royal icing until the whole of the cake is covered. Apply more if necessary.

8 Hold the metal side scraper firmly in your hand, with your fingers evenly spaced. Pay great attention to the pressure created by your little finger – if it is not strong enough, you will end up with sloping sides (also known as the 'lighthouse effect').

## Tip

The base of the side scraper should always touch the surface of the cake drum. If the angle of the side scraper to the surface of the cake is too acute, a smooth surface will not be achieved. If the angle is too obtuse, you will end up removing all the royal icing from the side of the cake.

9 Make sure that the piece of masking tape (or in this case, pin) on the side of the cake drum is level with the side scraper on the cake (at the 3 o'clock position). Firmly hold the side scraper against the side of the cake. With your other hand, take hold of the underneath edge of the turntable. This hand should be in advance of the hand holding the side scraper. It's important that the turntable is turned 360 degrees in one smooth, single action. If you stop turning, you will create a ridge on the side of the cake.

## Tip

For subsequent coats of royal icing on the cake side, you will start this scraping motion at 6 and 9 o'clock.

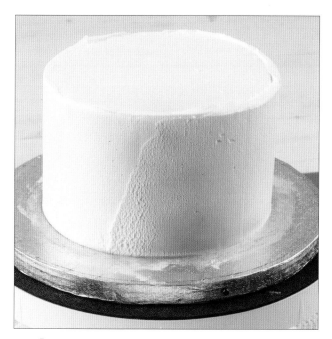

10 It is normal on a first coat to have the marzipan shining through the royal icing in places.

11 Remove the surplus royal icing from the top edge of the cake. Use small cutting actions with a palette knife with the blade running towards the centre of the cake, and level with the top rather than at an angle. The blade must be wiped clean with a clean, damp cloth with each action. Don't use a sweeping motion around the top edge of the cake, as this will cause problems for all additional coats.

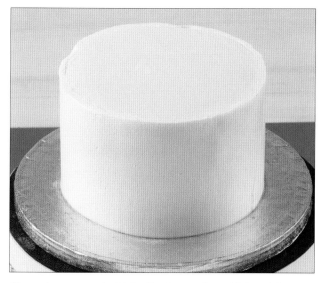

*The cake covered with its first layer of royal icing. It is important when working with royal icing to clean as you go, so wipe away any icing on the cake drum – do not allow this to dry. Leave the coated cake to dry (ideally for no less than eight hours) before removing the take-off mark on the side of the cake (left by the side scraper). Always use a plain knife for this purpose. Brush away all the dry particles of royal icing from the cake and board before continuing.*

## Subsequent coats

The second coat is exactly the same as the first, except that the mark made on the edge of the cake drum needs to be at the 9 o'clock position when removing the surplus royal icing with the knife. Leave this coat to dry (ideally no less than eight hours) before coating the side of the cake. Make sure that the marker on the cake drum is at the 6 o'clock position, when positioning the metal side scraper for smoothing the cake side.

Leave the coated cake to dry (ideally for no less than eight hours) before removing the take-off mark of the side scraper from the cake with the edge of a plain knife.

Brush away all the dry particles of royal icing from the cake and cake board before continuing. The third coat is the same as the second, except that the marker needs to be at the 12 o'clock position when smoothing the top and at 9 o'clock when positioning the metal side scraper for the cake side.

## Covering a cake with fondant (sugarpaste)

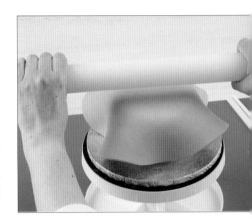

1 Rub a clear alcohol such as gin or vodka on the marzipan to sterilise it.

2 Roll out the fondant (sugarpaste) using space bars and as for the marzipan, drape it over the cake using the rolling pin, making sure the edge is touching the cake drum. Follow the steps on page 18, as for marzipan, to smooth and finish the cake.

## Covering a cake drum with fondant (sugarpaste) – the bandage method

An iced cake drum creates a more professional look to the finished celebration cake. Dampen the cake drum with water before beginning.

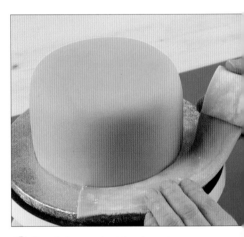

1 Roll a piece of fondant (sugarpaste) into a long sausage. Lightly dust the work surface with icing sugar (powdered sugar) and roll out the sausage until it is approx. 3mm ($\frac{1}{8}$in) thick. Cut one of the long edges straight.

2 Roll up the strip of fondant (sugarpaste) like a bandage.

3 Carefully unwind the bandage around the cake with the cut edge towards the cake. Ease it into position and don't unroll too much at once.

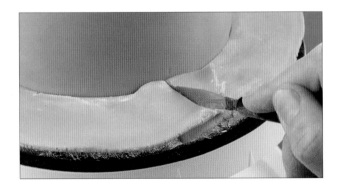

4 Overlap the fondant (sugarpaste) where it meets and cut through both layers. Remove the surplus and rub with your thumbs to smooth the join.

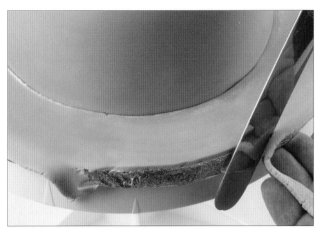

**5** Trim the fondant (sugarpaste) which is overhanging the cake drum.

### Option

At this stage, you can emboss the edge of the fondant (sugarpaste) on the cake drum with a design of your choice.

**6** Rub the cut edge around the edge of the cake drum with the side of your hand to smooth it.

### A square cake drum

A square cake drum is covered in exactly the same way – it is just a case of easing the rolled out fondant (sugarpaste) around the corners (there is no need to cut and create mitred corners).

### Making a chamfered cake drum

• Glue two cake drums together, for instance a 22.5cm and a 30cm (9in and 12in), with non-toxic glue. Make sure the smaller cake drum is central before leaving the glue to set.

• Wet the step on the cake drums with water.

• Roll a piece of fondant (sugarpaste) into a long sausage.

• Pack the step with the fondant (sugarpaste).

• Use a smoother to level and smooth the icing, creating an even angle all round.

• Trim the icing level with the edges of the cake drums.

• Leave to dry for twenty-four hours.

• Place the cake on the completed drum and coat it as normal, then coat the cake drum with royal icing or cover with fondant (sugarpaste). If the chamfered cake drum is to be coated with royal icing, follow the instructions for coating a regular cake drum with royal icing (pages 26–27), but use a flexi-scraper to smooth the royal icing instead of the metal side scraper.

# Piping

## Piping nozzle information

Different manufacturers label the piping nozzles in different ways when it comes to the size of the opening and the type (plain or serrated). For example, a PME No. 5 is a serrated nozzle, whereas a Wilton No. 5 is a plain round nozzle.

Most of the piping nozzles used in this book are Bekenal. The diameter of the opening on these tips are approximately as follows:

No. 0: 0.25mm ($\frac{1}{128}$in)

No. 1: 0.5mm ($\frac{1}{64}$in)

No. 1.5: 0.75mm ($\frac{1}{32}$in)

No. 2: 1mm ($\frac{1}{16}$in)

No. 3: 2.25mm ($\frac{3}{32}$in)

No. 4: 2.5mm ($\frac{5}{64}$in)

## Making a piping bag

Paper piping bags are essential for good piping. No less than four sizes are required. Baking parchment is a better choice than greaseproof paper.

- Cut a rectangular piece of baking parchment:

Size 1 (extra small): 25.4 x 15.2cm (10 x 6in)

Size 2 (small): 30.5 x 20.3cm (12 x 8in)

Size 3 (medium): 30.5 x 33cm (12 x 13in)

Size 4 (large) 45.7cm (18 x 15in)

- Fold the piece of paper in half diagonally to make a triangle (with one flat end – not pointed).

- Cut the paper along the fold line.

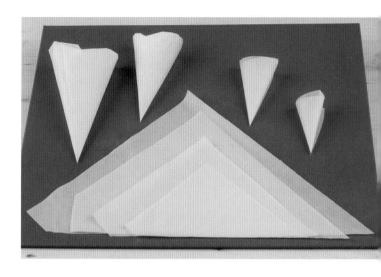

1 Take hold of one point of the triangle and hold the flat end between your index finger and thumb, with the paper over the outside of your hand. The long edge should be level with your fingertips and the short end pointing up your arm.

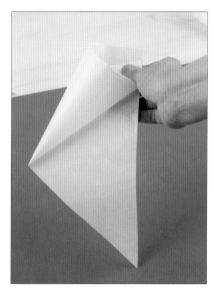

2 Take hold of the base point and wrap the paper around your hand, at the same time rotating your wrist. Bring the point up to meet the short point.

3 Take hold of the remaining point and wrap it round the cone, bringing it to meet the other points. Take this point slightly further around the cone; the amount depends on the diameter of the piping nozzle you are using, as the nozzle must fit the piping bag snugly.

**Tip**
It's important that all the layers lie smoothly on top of one another (if they don't, ease the layer around until they do).

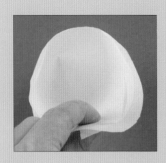

**Tip**

There should not be a gap at the point end; it should be sharp enough to prick the skin. If you can see through the point end, then you have created a weak piping bag, so adjust the layers of paper to close up the hole.

4 Fold the top points into the piping bag and make a firm crease. Make a 5mm (¼in) cut through all the layers.

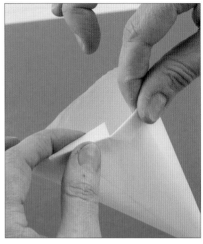

5 Fold and firmly crease one side of the cut towards the inside of the piping bag and the other side towards the outside.

## Making a piping bag fit the nozzle

When cutting off the pointed end of a piping bag ready for the nozzle, it is important that you cut off the right amount – too little and icing will be able to travel down the outside of the piping nozzle and ooze out of the opening. Too much and as soon as you apply any pressure to the piping bag, the nozzle will fall out. Normally the ideal amount is just less than 1cm (³/₈in) but this does depend on the make and type of piping nozzle. Some piping nozzles are short, so cutting off the normal amount could mean that the nozzle will fall out once pressure is applied.

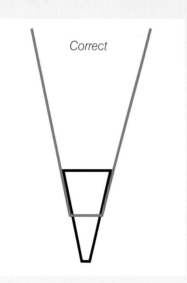

*Correct*

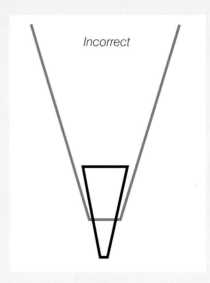

*Incorrect*

## Paddling and colouring royal icing

The reason for paddling royal icing is to break down the size and number of air pockets (bubbles), which can cause a piped line to break.

1 If only a small quantity of coloured royal icing is required (for one piping bag) then instead of colouring the icing in a bowl, add a drop of liquid food colour to the royal icing on a side scraper.

2 Paddle the royal icing with a backwards and forwards action with a palette knife. This will not only break down the air pockets but it will also mix in the food colour.

## Filling a small piping bag

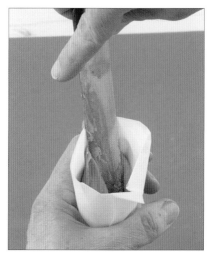

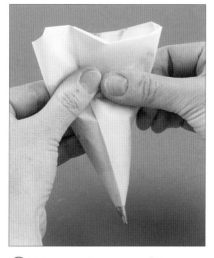

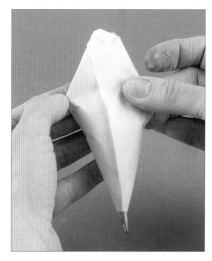

1 Collect the paddled royal icing on the tip of the knife blade. Insert the tip of the knife into the piping bag and scrape off the royal icing by running the blade against the hand holding the piping bag, through the paper.

2 Make sure the seam of the piping bag is central and squeeze the royal icing down the bag using your index fingers and thumbs.

3 Fold the corners of the piping bag down, away from the seam.

4 Fold the top down two or three times, away from the seam, to make a nice, neat parcel.

## Filling a medium or large piping bag

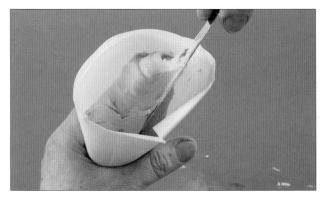

1 Paddle the required amount of royal icing with a palette knife on a clean work surface, mixing in food colour at the same time (if required).

2 Collect the paddled royal icing on the tip of the knife blade. Insert the tip of the knife into the piping bag and scrape off the royal icing by running the blade against your hand through the paper of the piping bag.

## How to hold a piping bag
The way you hold the piping bag depends on its size.

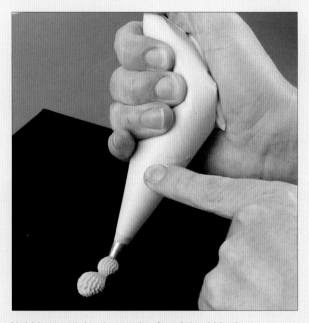

When using a small size 1 or 2 piping bag, hold it the same way as you would a pen, between index finger and middle finger. Apply pressure with the tip of your thumb.

Hold larger piping bags, size 3 and 4, within the hand, and apply pressure from the base of your thumb (metacarpal).

- Everyone's hands shake, so when piping, use a guide finger – the index finger of your other, non-dominant hand, to touch the piping bag as you pipe. One shake counteracts the other and this steadies the piping action.
- It is important to keep winding the piping bag down as you work – so that it remains nice and firm – if it is allowed to go soft, it will become harder to control the piping.

## Sieving royal icing

A knee high (or pop sock) is used to sieve the royal icing when using fine piping nozzles such as 00, 0 and 1 as a minute particle can cause the tip to block. Paddle the royal icing in the normal way on a side scaper. Use approx. 15ml (1 tablespoon).

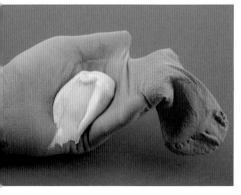

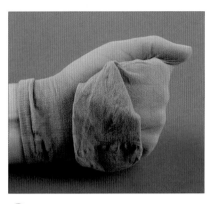

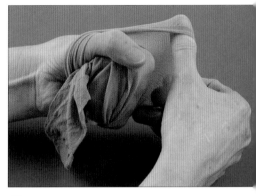

1 Insert your left hand into the top of the knee high, with the elastic section round your wrist. Place the paddled royal icing on the palm of your left hand.

2 Close your fingers over the royal icing and hold it there.

3 With your right hand, carefully pull the elasticated section off your left hand, over the royal icing you are grasping.

4 Release the fingers on your left hand. The royal icing will be incased in the knee high, as shown.

5 Carefully drop the knee high section with the royal icing into the prepared piping bag. Using your index fingers and thumbs, work the royal icing down the piping bag.

6 Hold the piping bag firmly with the index finger and thumb of your left hand and pull the knee high out of the piping bag using your right hand as shown. Fold the piping bag down and pipe in the normal way.

## Piping a line

• Touch the surface with the piping nozzle to start.

• Apply pressure to the piping bag.

• As soon as you see the icing emerging, lift the piping bag away from the surface.

• Continue applying pressure to the piping bag as you move it away, keeping the line taut.

• Once the line is long enough, ease the pressure off.

• Touch the surface again to break the line.

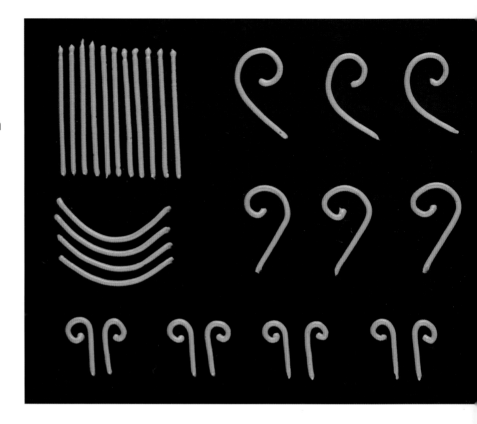

To help my students I teach them a little tune to go with the instructions to pipe a line:

Touch to start, apply the pressure, lift, ease the pressure, off and down.

### Troubleshooting tips

• If you stay too long before you lift the piping bag away from the surface, you will create a hammer-head or bulbous end to the line.

• If the piped line snaps, it is due to one of the following:

1 You did not apply enough pressure as you moved the piping bag away from the surface.

2 There is an air pocket, meaning that you did not paddle the royal icing sufficiently.

3 The piping nozzle is blocked by hard lumps in the royal icing.

• If the line is uneven in shape, this suggests that the nozzle was dragged across the surface of the cake instead of lifting the piping bag. If you did lift the piping bag away from the surface, this suggests that you applied too much pressure to the piping bag and so lost control of the line.

• If there is a point standing to attention at the end of the piped line, this suggests that you were still applying pressure to the piping bag once it touched the surface.

## Piping dots and bulbs

Dots and bulbs are always created with a plain round nozzle, the most common sizes being 0–4. Royal icing used for dots and bulbs needs to be a fraction softer than that which you would use to pipe a shell or snail's trail, as there should be no lines on the finished shape. Add a couple of drops of water when paddling the royal icing before filling the correct size piping bag.

• Hold the piping bag at a 90 degree angle to the surface of the icing on the cake.

• Touch the surface to start, and apply the pressure.

• As soon as you see the icing, move the tip of the nozzle a fraction off the surface, keeping it in the icing, and allow the royal icing to puff up around the nozzle.

• Keep applying a steady pressure to the piping bag as you gradually move the nozzle a few more fractions away from the cake surface.

• When the desired size is reached, stop applying pressure to the piping bag and at the same time quickly twist and flick it to the right.

• If it is just a piped dot, then the tiny take-off mark is normally left, unless this is a competition piece. However if it is a bulb, made with a larger nozzle, the take-off mark is normally blended and tidied up with a damp paintbrush.

### The perfect bulb

Ideally a piped bulb should be a perfect sphere with no visible ridges or take-off mark. This might sound simple, but a perfect bulb is classed as the hardest thing to pipe. To the best of my knowledge, the best royal icer the UK has ever produced was Ronnie Rock, who died at the age of 42 in 1958. His piped bulbs were flawless.

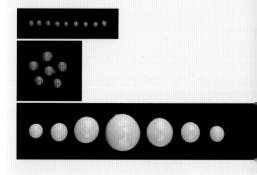

## Piping a teardrop: shell and snail's trail

The technique for creating a shell border is the same as piping a snail's trail, except that you use a serrated piping nozzle for a shell rather than the plain one used for a snail's trail.

• Hold the piping bag at a 35 degree angle to the surface. Touch the surface to start.

• Apply pressure as soon as you see the icing coming out of the piping nozzle. Lift it a tiny fraction (1mm or $1/_{32}$in) from the surface.

• Hold the piping nozzle in the same place, but continue to apply the pressure, allowing the royal icing to puff up and move a fraction backward.

• Once the required size has been achieved, reduce the pressure on the piping bag as you pull it along the surface of the cake – causing the icing to snap and create a point. You should have created a beautiful teardrop shape.

• The point should be horizontal; if it is pointing upwards, it suggests that on pulling away, you lifted the piping bag up.

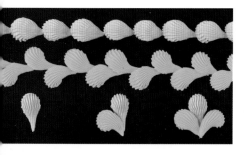

To help my students I teach them a little tune to go with the instruction:

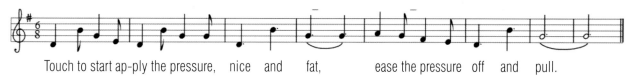

Touch to start ap-ply the pressure, nice and fat, ease the pressure off and pull.

## Piping 'S' and 'C' scrolls

There are two types of scroll, which can be traced back to the royal icing founders: a rope scroll and an agitated scroll.

• Hold the piping bag at a 35 degree angle to the cake surface. If you are working along the top edge of the cake, the scroll will start on the top, move down onto the side and finish on the top, hiding the corner edge.

• Agitated scroll – Touch the surface and apply pressure to the piping bag. Keep the tip of the nozzle in the piped icing while you make tiny circular motions with the piping bag. The final shape tapers from broad at one end, coming to a point at the other.

• Rope scroll – Touch the surface and apply pressure to the piping bag, while moving it in a circular motion, keeping the tip of the nozzle visible. The final shape tapers from broad at one end, coming to a point at the other.

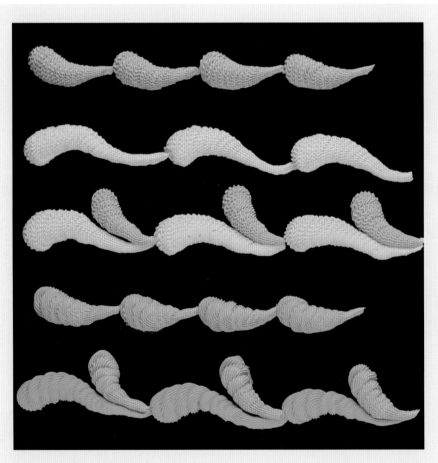

*Agitated 'C' scrolls.*

*Agitated 'S' scrolls.*

*Agitated 'S' and 'C' scrolls.*

*Rope 'C' scrolls.*

*Rope 'S' and 'C' scrolls.*

# Run sugar

Run-outs are pieces which have been created with run sugar (royal icing that has been let down with water till it flows). Place a small amount of fresh royal icing in a bowl and add a tiny amount of water while stirring with a knife. Continue to add water until the royal icing flows. To test for the right consistency, leave a trail of run sugar on the surface of the run sugar in the bowl; the trail needs to disappear in a set amount of time. The length of time for the trail to disappear depends on the style of run-out being created – for flat run-outs, the trail needs to be visible at five seconds, but disappear by seven seconds. Low relief run-outs need a thicker run sugar consistency, and high relief requires the run sugar to be thicker again.

Cover the bowl with a damp cloth and leave it to stand for thirty minutes. Cut though the bubbles on the surface of the run sugar with a knife. Pour run sugar into a size 3 piping bag to half fill it. Wind the piping bag down in the normal way to create a neat parcel. Snip the tip off the piping bag carefully – the larger the opening, the less control you have of the run sugar, and if it is too large, any air pockets still in the run sugar will not pop as it passes through the opening. Don't make the hole any larger than a No. 1.5 nozzle on a size 3 piping bag.

There are three types of run-out:

**Flat** – the outline is always visible. This style tends to be associated with royal icer Nadene Hurst, who was well known for her beautiful decoupage run-out designs.

**Low relief** – the outline is hidden. As the name implies, these run-outs are very slightly domed.

**High relief** – no outline is used. The reason for outlining a run-out is not to hold the run sugar in, but to stop it from shrinking back. Therefore the high relief style requires the consistency of the royal icing to be spot on – too soft and it will not hold the shape, too firm and there will be visible marks on the surface of the finished piece.

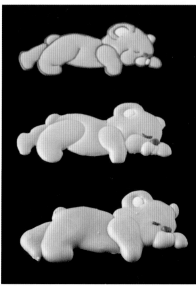

*From top to bottom: flat, low relief and high relief run sugar bears.*

Run-outs should have a high gloss finish, which is achieved by drying the surface of the run sugar as quickly as possible once flooded, under an anglepoise lamp with a 60 watt bulb, which gives off a small amount of heat. Note that energy efficient bulbs will not generate enough heat to dry a run-out. The run-out needs to be under this heat source for at least fifteen minutes, and then it needs to be transferred to the drying environment. In years gone by, this would have meant an airing cupboard, but most homes no longer have this. The modern alternative is a food dehydrator. The temperature setting on the food dehydrator will vary slightly between the various manufacturers, but it should be somewhere between 35–46°C (95–115°F). All run-outs, no matter what their size - should be dry within twenty-four hours. If they are not, it suggests that the royal icing was too old or wrongly made i.e. a heavy mass, or the drying environment was wrong.

If a run sugar piece has been dried in the correct environment, the back should also have a gloss finish.

It is important that a run sugar piece is made on the right covering material: wax paper or food grade acetate (butcher's wrap). Any other material might shrink and distort under the heat from the lamp.

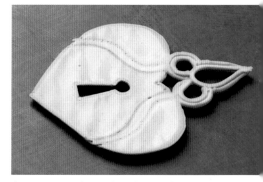

*A run sugar piece showing a gloss on the back which suggests that it is strong.*

# Making piped roses

When piping roses, it is best to work on several at the same time, as this allows a small amount of drying time between layers. You will need a no. 57 petal nozzle, but if you are left-handed, make sure it is a left-handed nozzle, and reverse the direction for turning the cocktail stick (so clockwise becomes anticlockwise).

**You will need**

Piping bag (size 3)
No. 57 nozzle
Cocktail sticks
Wax paper

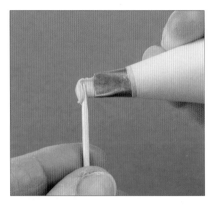

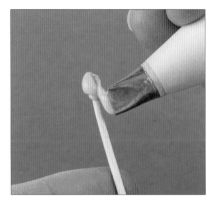

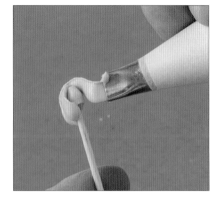

1 Hold the piping bag in one hand and a cocktail stick in the other. The narrow end of the nozzle needs to be at a fraction higher than the tip of the cocktail stick. Touch the cocktail stick to start and apply pressure to the piping bag, turning the cocktail stick at the same time. Pipe a tight spiral (it should not have an open centre).

2 To finish the spiral, bring the nozzle down in a sweeping action and finish on the cocktail stick.

3 Pipe the next petal (one of three). Touch the cocktail stick to start each petal. In a clockwise direction, pipe the petal in a horse-shoe shape while slowly turning the cocktail stick. Finish the petal by touching the cocktail stick.

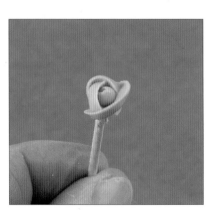

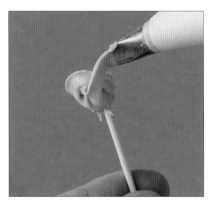

4 Repeat step 3 with the remaining two petals. Each petal should overlap the previous one and the last petal should overlap the first.

5 Pipe the next five petals in the same way as the previous three, but this time in an anticlockwise direction.

*The completed rose.*

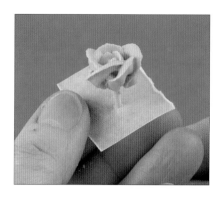

6 Feed the cocktail stick through a small square of wax paper and remove the rose.

7 Leave the roses to dry completely.

## Making a leaf nozzle and piping the calyx

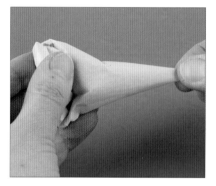

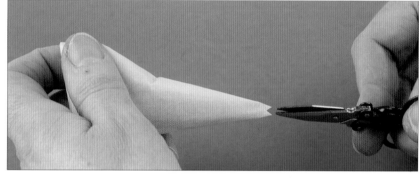

8 Create a piping bag (size 2) but give it an extra half twist to make it narrower. Half fill it with royal icing which has been coloured green. Fold the top of the piping bag over as normal to make a neat, tidy parcel. Squash the tip of the piping bag flat with your index finger and thumb.

9 Using fine scissors, cut a small inverted 'V' from the tip of the piping bag.

10 Pipe five small leaf shapes on the base of the piped rose to create the calyx. Leave to dry.

*The finished piped rose with its calyx.*

# ROSE BASKET

In this project you will learn how to make marzipan roses, spilling out of a basket made from a royal-icing-coated cake. There are various possibilities with basketweave designs. The rose basket is made with the classic technique, using a flat serrated nozzle and a plain round nozzle. A few more styles of basketweave are shown at the end of this project in case you are inspired to to branch out.

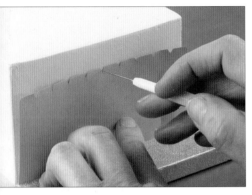

1 Create a paper template the same size as one side of the cake and divide it into an even number of sections approx. 13mm (½in) apart. Use a scriber to mark these sections onto the side of the cake.

2 Use a set square to scribe vertical lines on the cake sides to create the sections. Coat the cake drum with royal icing (see pages 26–27). Leave to dry for eight hours. Place a No. 22 basketweave nozzle in a large piping bag (size 4). Paddle a quantity of cream-coloured royal icing on the work surface and half fill the piping bag. Place a No. 3 nozzle in a size 3 piping bag. Half fill the piping bag with royal icing coloured brown.

3 Place the cake on a cake tilter. Using the No. 3 nozzle, pipe a line directly on top of one of the scribed lines (start at the top edge of the cake and finish at the base). If necessary, use a damp paintbrush to correct the line and neaten the take-off point. Starting at the top edge of the cake, pipe a short horizontal line using the No. 22 nozzle from the scribed line before the vertical piped line to the scribed line after it. Leave a gap the width of the nozzle and repeat down the side of the cake.

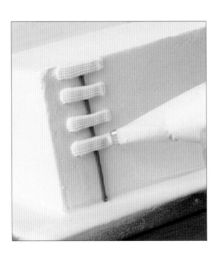

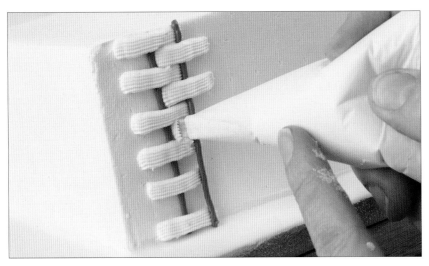

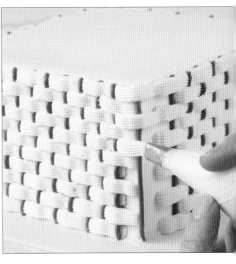

4 Pipe another brown vertical line with the No. 3 nozzle on the next scribed line, to the right of the previous vertical line and going over the No. 22 horizontal piped lines. Using the No. 22 nozzle, pipe a short horizontal line in the gap, starting at the side of the first brown vertical line and lifting it over the second. Finish at the scribed line to the right of the brown vertical line.

5 Repeat until the cake sides are completely piped.

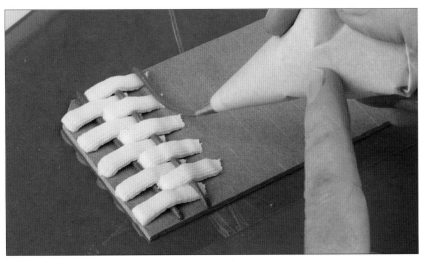

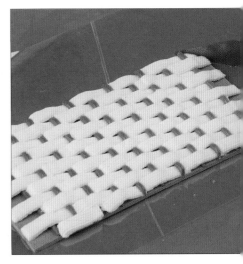

6 Take a cake board the same size as the top of the cake and cut it in half. Cut across the two top corners. Scribe vertical lines on the underside (not the silver side). Pipe a basketweave design for the basket lid.

7 Clean up the edges of the lid if necessary using an artist's palette knife. Leave to dry.

8 Divide the cake top into two equal portions using the scriber and a ruler.

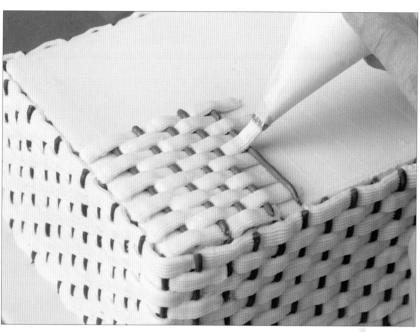

9 Scribe vertical lines in the same way as on the cake sides, on one half of the top.

10 Pipe a basketweave as before over half the cake top.

11 Place a No. 43 nozzle in a size 3 piping bag. Half fill the piping bag with royal icing, coloured brown. Pipe a line around the top edge of the cake, half on the top and half on the side, to hide the join. Leave to dry.

12 Place the basket lid on a piece of food-grade acetate and pipe a line in the same way around three sides. Leave to dry for no less than four hours.

## Marzipan roses

These are pulled roses – in other words they are produced without using a cutter. While the icing is drying, create the marzipan roses and leaves. Colour the marzipan with fuchsia paste food colour.

**Tip**
When working with marzipan, it is easier if you keep a film of water on your hands. Keep wiping your hands on a damp cloth. No glue is required, as marzipan sticks to itself.

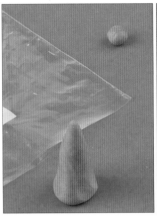

**13** Take a walnut-sized piece of marzipan and roll it into a ball and then a cone. Place six small balls of marzipan 13mm (½in) across, in a good quality plastic food bag. Use your thumb to flatten them. Thin the top edge with your index finger, leaving the base of the petal thick. When removing the flattened balls from the bag, pick them up by their thickest edge.

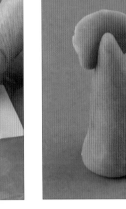
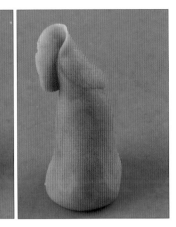

**14** Position the first petal 3mm (⅛in) above the tip of the cone. Tightly wrap the first petal around the cone, one side at a time.

**15** When looking down on to this first petal, you should not be able to see the tip of the cone shape. Attach a further two petals to the cone, interleaving them – the right-hand side of the front petal should be tucked in first.

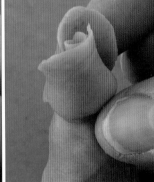

**16** Attach a further three petals to the cone, interleaving as before.

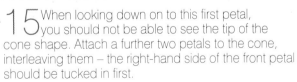

50

## Marzipan leaves

Colour the marzipan with spruce green paste food colour for these pulled leaves.

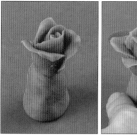

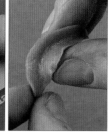

*The finished marzipan rose and leaf.*

17 For a larger rose, make five more petals and attach them to the cone, again interleaving them. Gently press the cone with your index fingers and thumbs where the last petals were attached, to create a rounded base of the rose. Cut the rose from the cone.

18 Take a large pea-sized piece of marzipan and roll it into a ball and then a double-ended cone. Place it in a plastic food bag and use your thumb to flatten it. Thin the side edges with your index finger. Remove the leaf from the bag, pinch it to make a central vein and then place it on a piece of crumpled foil to firm up.

## Completing the basket

19 Place a No. 1 nozzle in a small piping bag (size 2). Take sufficient royal icing (coloured brown) to half fill the piping bag. Paddle on a side scraper and then sieve using a knee high (see page 39) and fill the piping bag. Pipe lines over the brown basket edging at a 45 degree angle, keeping the lines as close as possible.

20 Secure the marzipan roses and leaves to the top of the cake using cream-coloured royal icing.

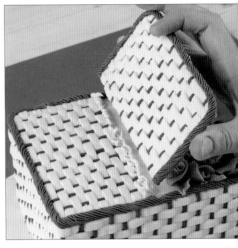

21 Keep checking (with the lid) that you have not over-filled the top of the cake with the marzipan roses and leaves.

22 Once you are happy that you have enough roses and leaves, pipe a line of cream-coloured royal icing and secure the basket lid. Use a damp paintbrush to neaten the join.

23 Make a double flat bow. Cut four lengths of ribbon: 14cm (5½in), 23cm (9in), 17.8cm (7in) and 3cm (1¼in). Place a small piece of double-sided sticky tape on one end of the 23cm (9in) length and attach the opposite end to make a loop. Repeat with the 17.8cm (7in) length. Place a piece of the tape inside each loop at the join, ensure that the join is central and press the loop to create a figure '8'. Repeat with the smaller loop. Secure the larger loop centrally on the 14cm (5½in) strip of ribbon. Place another piece of double-sided tape centrally on the 23cm (9in) loop and attach the 17.8cm (7in) loop.

24 Attach a small piece of double-sided tape at the central point on the loops and secure the last piece of ribbon. Wrap this small piece round the bow and secure with tape at the back.

25 Secure the bow to the cake with cream-coloured royal icing. To finish the cake, attach a 13mm (½in) satin ribbon to the edge of the cake drum using non-toxic glue stick. Overlap the ribbon at the back of the cake by 13mm (½in).

*A detail of the finished cake.*

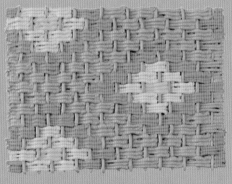

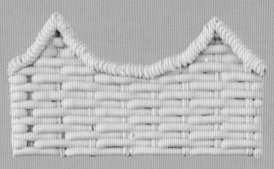

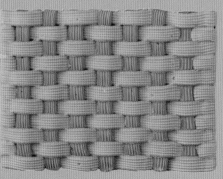

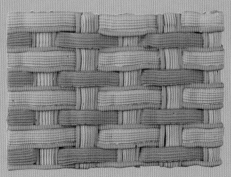

*Further examples of basketweave designs that you can make with piping.*

# FLOWER BORDER

This beautiful floral design is piped onto a cake covered in sky-blue fondant (sugarpaste), giving the impression of a glorious summer's day – perfect for a summer birthday or a keen gardener. The border design repeats three times around the cake, and you will learn how to create a template for this using cash register receipt roll. To begin, create the piped roses with pale pink royal icing and the No. 57 nozzle (see page 44). Cover the cake with the blue fondant (sugarpaste), then cover the visible part of cake drum with green fondant (sugarpaste) using the bandage method (see page 32). Ideally, leave the cake covering to skin over before continuing with the decoration.

## You will need

17.5cm (7in) round cake, 7.5cm (3in) deep

25cm (10in) cake drum

650g (1lb 5oz) blue fondant (sugarpaste) slightly marbled (not completely mixed)

150g (5oz) green fondant (sugarpaste)

30g (1oz) pale brown fondant (sugarpaste)

454g (1lb) royal icing

Piping nozzles No. 0, No. 1 (x 4), No.s 1.5, 2 and 57

Piping bags size 1, 2 and 3

Grass piping nozzle (Wilton 122)

Nozzle adapter

Piece of sponge for texture

30cm (12in) disposable piping bag

Edible liquid food colours (droplet): blue, buttercup, chocolate, fern green, fuchsia, grape violet, and holly green

Plastic side scraper

Palette knife

Sable paintbrush No. 2

Scriber

Scissors

Cash register receipt roll

Masking tape

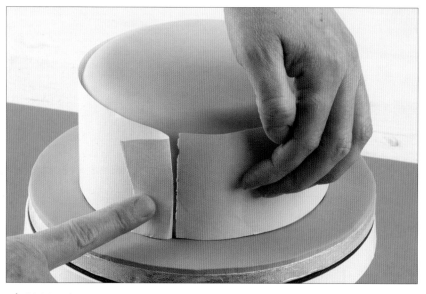

1 Divide the cake into three equal sections. The easiest way is to take a length of cash register receipt roll, wrap it around the cake and fold the end over where it meets, leaving 13mm (½in) of paper beyond the fold. Cut off the excess paper.

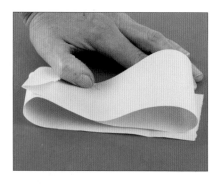

2 Fold the length of paper into three sections, not including the folded-back end. Cut out a tiny piece of paper at the base corners to mark the sections.

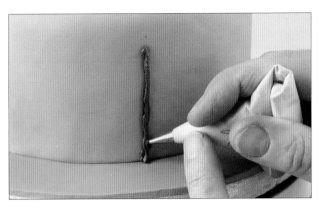

3 Wrap the strip of paper around the cake (cut-out bits to the base) and secure the ends together with masking tape. The extra 13mm (½in) is to give you an overlap i.e. to create a bit of ease should you need it. Use a scriber to mark the sections.

4 Fill a size 2 piping bag (No. 2 nozzle) with royal icing that has been coloured chocolate brown. Pipe a stem for the standard rose bush at each of the scribed marks. The stem is supposed to have an uneven finish.

5 To pipe the rose bush's leaves, create a size 3 piping bag with the tip cut for piping leaves, as shown on page 45. Half fill with royal icing coloured with a mixture of fern green and holly green liquid food colour. Use this to pipe the leaves on the standard rose bush.

6 While the leaves are still wet, attach the piped roses.

7 Next, create the lupins. Pipe the stem first using a size 1 piping bag (No. 1 nozzle) and green royal icing. Pipe the flowers with a size 2 piping bag (No 1.5 nozzle) and violet royal icing, starting 2cm (¾in) from the base of the stem. Pipe a row of small teardrops at a slight angle, facing towards the stem, with the narrow point touching the stem. Repeat on the other side of the stem. Make three stems of lupins.

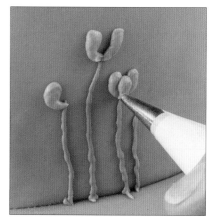

8 Complete the lupin flowers by piping another row of teardrops on top of the green stem, finishing with a few graduated dots at the top of the stem.

9 For the tulips, pipe the stems with a size 1 piping bag (No. 1 nozzle) and holly green royal icing. The flowers are created by piping three teardrops from a size 2 piping bag (No. 2 nozzle) and fuchsia royal icing. To create the bottom of the tulip, curve the base of the point on the first two teardrops. The central teardrops should start a fraction lower than the top of the first two teardrops.

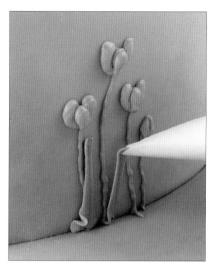

10 Add a tulip bud. Create another piping bag for piping leaves (see page 45). Half fill it with royal icing coloured with holly green food colour. Pipe the leaves for the tulips. Starting at the base, squeeze out the royal icing to the required height, then lay it on the cake side.

11 Fill a size 1 piping bag (No. 1 nozzle) with fern green royal icing and pipe the stems for the daisies. Half fill two piping bags (No. 1 nozzles), one with white royal icing, and one with buttercup. Pipe five tiny white teardrops to create a daisy, then pipe a yellow dot in the centre.

12 Pipe green teardrops with a No. 1 nozzle to create the leaves.

13 For the yellow flowers under the standard rose bush, pipe another group of stems and leaves with the fern green royal icing, using a No. 1 nozzle. Create the flowers by piping a group of three teardrops with buttercup royal icing and the No. 1 nozzle.

14 Pipe a small green teardrop at the base of the yellow flower to create the calyx.

15 To create the forget-me-nots, pipe a group of long teardrops to create the leaves using a No. 1 nozzle and holly green royal icing. Pull the tip of the scriber through each leaf, base to tip, to create the midrib. Half fill a size 1 piping bag (No. 0 nozzle) with blue royal icing. Pipe a row of dots between each leaf.

*Opposite*
*Detail of the finished cake.*

16 Spread some green royal icing on the covered cake drum using the palette knife. Use a piece of sponge to create a texture. Keep turning the piece of sponge around, as if it becomes too damp, it will create spikes of royal icing rather than a fine texture.

17 Use the adapter to attach the grass nozzle to the disposable piping bag and then half fill with green royal icing. Pipe grass around the base of the cake. It is important not to touch the surface of the cake or drum with the grass nozzle, so squeeze the piping bag and let the piped lines drop onto the surface, then stop applying the pressure and then give it a quick flick (with your wrist) to snap the piped lines.

18 Create a few pebbles with the pale brown fondant (sugarpaste) and position at random on the cake drum.

# ENGAGEMENT HEART

This romantic cake has a traditional feel even though it is covered with fondant (sugarpaste) rather than royal icing. It is then piped with a delicate flower design in subtle colours. You will learn how to create a template for the cake sides to help you to pipe the scalloped design. Marzipan the cake before covering it with white fondant (sugarpaste). Cover the cake drum with the same. If possible, allow the covering to skin over before continuing.

## You will need

17.5cm (7in) heart-shaped cake, 7.5cm (3in) deep

25cm (10in) heart-shaped cake drum

750g (1½lb) white fondant (sugarpaste)

240g (8oz) royal icing

Droplet liquid food colour in buttercup, fuchsia, fern, holly green and grape violet

Piping nozzles No. 2, No. 1 (x 3) and No. 0

Piping bags size 1 and 2

Scriber

15mm (½in) satin ribbon

Non-toxic glue stick

Cash register receipt roll

Masking tape

Optional: FMM embosser (scroll set 1) for edge of iced cake drum

Scissors

Knee high (pop sock)

1 Make a paper template for the side of the cake. Take a strip of cash register receipt roll the same length as the cake plus 13mm (½in). Divide and fold it into five equal sections, without incorporating the extra bit. Fold the folded paper in half again and draw then cut a half scallop. Unfold the length of paper and wrap it round the cake. Secure the ends together with a piece of masking tape. The extra bit is to give you an overlap i.e. create a bit of ease. Place a small bottle or something similar between the lobes of the heart to keep the template in place.

**Tip**

Work on the piping details for all five sections at the same time, to keep each piped section even in size.

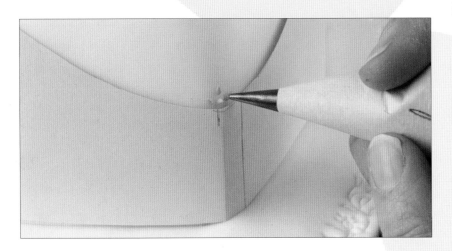

2 Half fill a size 1 piping bag (No. 1 nozzle) with buttercup-coloured royal icing. Using the paper template as a guide, pipe a tiny yellow dot at the central point on each of the scallops. Be careful not to pipe on the paper template. Half fill a size 1 piping bag (No. 1 nozzle) with fuchsia-coloured royal icing. Pipe half of the flower (three tiny teardrops) around the yellow dot. Ensure the piped petals do not touch the central dot.

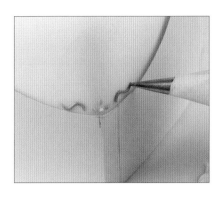

**3** Half fill a size 1 piping bag (No. 1 nozzle) with green-coloured royal icing. Pipe a small wavy line either side of the flower, keeping them even in size.

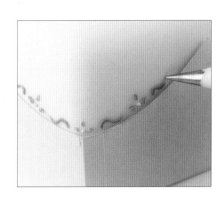

**4** Pipe another half flower (yellow dot and three teardrops) either side of the wavy lines, then add more wavy lines as shown.

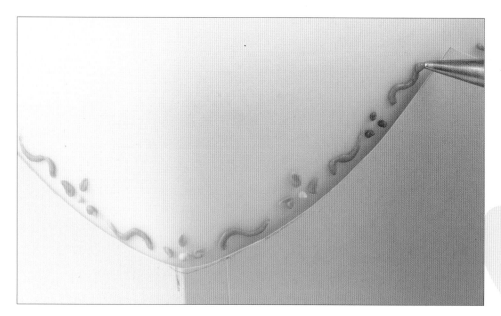

5 Half fill a size 1 piping bag (No. 0 nozzle) with grape violet-coloured royal icing. Don't forget to use a knee high to sieve the royal icing. Pipe a group of three dots. Finish with another wavy line.

6 Remove the paper template and complete the side design by finishing off the flowers, and piping the final wavy line. Pipe small teardrops for leaves either side of each wavy green line.

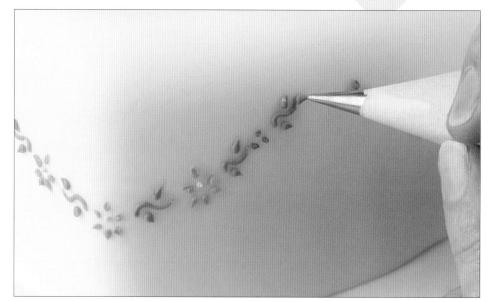

7 Use the size 1 piping bag (No. 0 nozzle) with grape violet-coloured royal icing to pipe curved clusters of dots, suggesting hanging blossoms. Ensure the shapes curve towards the centre of the design.

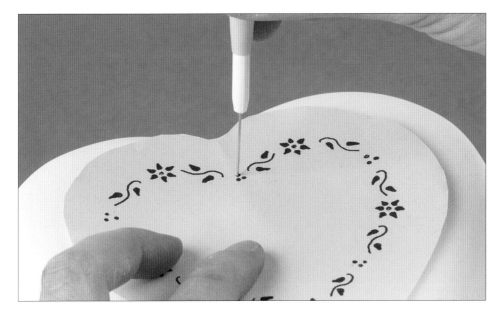

8 Transfer the heart template on page 123 onto paper and place it centrally on top of the cake. Use a scriber to transfer the basic shape by pin-pricking the centre of each flower and one of each of the groups of three dots. Remove the paper template.

9 Pipe a tiny dot of buttercup royal icing on top of each flower pin prick. Pipe a group of three grape-violet-coloured dots at the other pin prick marks.

10 Pipe six tiny pale pink teardrops around each of the yellow dots, without touching the dots, to create flowers.

**11** Pipe a small green wavy line between the piped flowers and the groups of three dots.

**12** Pipe two small teardrops for leaves, one each side of each wavy line. Half fill a size 2 piping bag (No. 2 nozzle) with white royal icing. Freehand pipe the inscription in the centre of the heart and then overpipe in a colour of your choice, using a No. 1 nozzle.

### Piping letters freehand

It is always a good idea to practise piping the required letters on the work surface first; this allows you to get an idea of the size and a feel for the movement which will be required. Do not drag the nozzle over the surface – allow the piped line to drop onto the surface. If necessary, a small amount of correction of the letter shape can be made with a damp paintbrush.

**13** Pipe a snail's trail around the base of the cake with the same nozzle and white royal icing. To finish, attach a 15mm (½in) satin ribbon to the edge of the cake drum using a non-toxic glue stick.

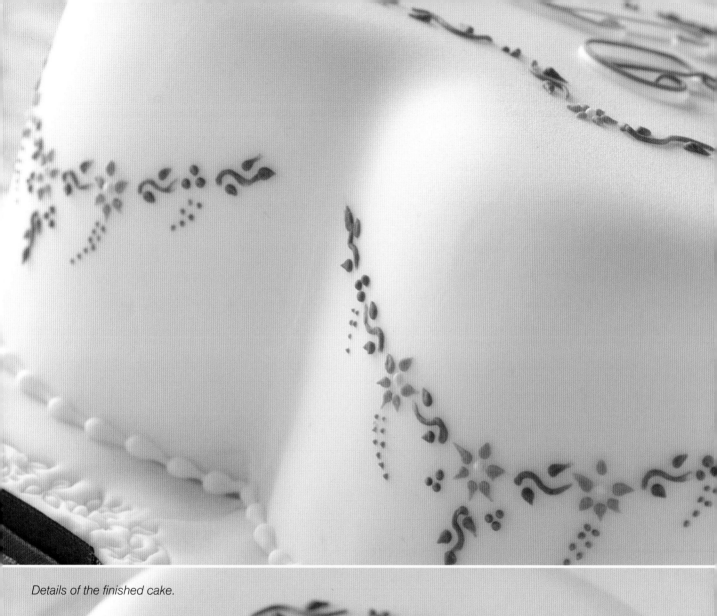

*Details of the finished cake.*

# WHITE DELIGHT

This stunning white cake with its delicate decorations would be perfect for a christening. You will learn scratch-piped embroidery, the window method of inscription and how to make beautiful lace pieces. Place the cake on the smaller cake drum, marzipan it, then apply three coats of royal icing to the top and sides. Coat the cake drum (see pages 26–27).Once this has dried, attach the satin ribbon to the edge using the glue stick. Glue the larger cake drum underneath, then coat the part you can see with royal icing. Leave to dry.

## You will need

20 x 15cm (8 x 6in) oval cake, 7.5cm (3in) deep

Stepped cake drums: 28.5 x 22.5cm (11 x 9in) and 33 x 18.5cm (13 x 11in)

1kg (2lbs) natural (white) marzipan

68g (1½lb) white royal icing with glycerine added for coating

240g (½lb) white royal icing for piping

Small amount of white vegetable fat

Piping nozzles No.s 0, 1 and 2

Piping bags size 1 and 2

Sable paintbrush No. 2

Scriber

Artist's palette knife

Turntable

Cake tilter

Sheet of perspex (plexiglass)

Food-grade acetate (butcher's wrap)

Masking tape

Cash register receipt roll

13mm (½in) double satin ribbon

Non-toxic glue stick

Small pieces of sponge foam

Stamen cottons (optional)

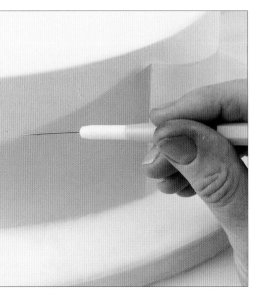

1 Wrap a strip of cash register receipt roll around the cake and fold it over where it meets. Cut the strip 13mm (½in) beyond the fold. Remove the strip, lay it flat and draw, then cut an elongated scallop (do not include the overlap). Wrap the strip around the cake, open up the overlap and secure with a piece of masking tape. Scribe the scallop line on to the cake.

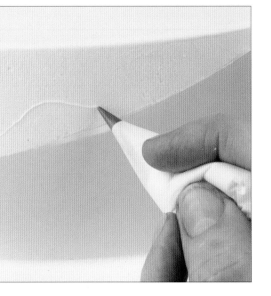

2 Fill a size 1 piping bag (No. 0 nozzle) with white royal icing. Tilt the cake. Freehand pipe the embroidery design a fraction above the scribed line. Start by piping a continuous wavy line around the cake, dragging the nozzle along the surface of the cake as you go. This is called scratch-piped embroidery.

66

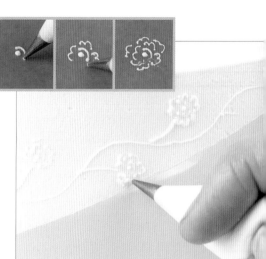

**3** At evenly spaced intervals, pipe branches coming off the wavy line.

**4** Next, pipe the roses. Start with a dot and then a 'c', then pipe '3's around the central dot for petals. This is shown on a coloured surface for clarity, but of course pipe directly onto the cake.

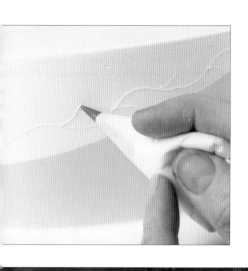

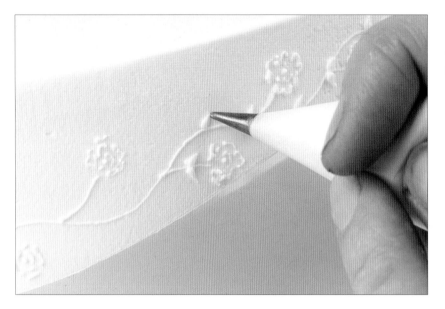

5 Add teardrop shapes for leaves in pairs on either side of the scratch-piped stems.

6 Continue piping the pattern around all the scallops, then remove the paper template.

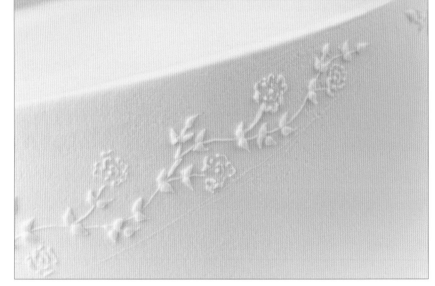

7 Pipe a regular snail's trail with a No. 2 nozzle around the base of the cake and the second cake drum. Overpipe the snail's trail on the base cake drum with a No. 0 nozzle, with 'S'-shaped lines as shown.

**8** Pipe the inscription using the window method. This is ideal for a single word or short, one-line inscription. Prepare a paper 'window' as shown, with the text written in and guide lines marked between each letter. Pipe the word(s) using a No. 1 nozzle, using your written text and guide lines to help you.

**9** Use an artist's palette knife to remove part of the piped line of the first letter. This is to allow for the insertion of a scratch-piped rose. Pipe the roses and leaves as shown in this detail from the finished cake (inset), crossing over the lettering in the places you have cleared.

**10** Pipe an alternating snail's trail with a No. 2 nozzle around the top edge of the cake.

## Lace pieces

The general rule with lace pieces is that the more times the piped lines touch each other, the stronger the piece. The bigger the lace pieces, the higher the number of breakages you should expect while releasing or handling them. Always pipe more than you need, allowing for breakage of one in every three for small lace pieces.

Secure a piece of food-grade acetate or wax paper to a sheet of perspex (plexiglass) or a flat board.

Apply a tiny amount of white vegetable fat to the acetate and then wipe it off. Take another clean piece of kitchen paper and wipe the surface of the acetate again (if there is too much white fat on the surface, it will break down the royal icing).

11 Slide the lace template for the hearts (see page 123) under the acetate. Fill a size 1 piping bag (No. 0 nozzle). Pipe around seventy-five lace hearts to allow for breakage, as this cake requires about fifty. If necessary, use a damp paintbrush to correct or neaten them. Providing your royal icing is of the right consistency, the lace pieces should be dry in thirty minutes. Do not use royal icing that is more than two days old for this purpose. Use an artist's palette knife to release the lace pieces from the acetate.

12 Attach each lace piece to the surface of the cake, beneath the scratch-piped embroidery design, with two tiny dots of royal icing.

13 Pipe the wings for the lace butterfly in the same way (see the template on page 123). Then pipe a body for the butterfly on the acetate. Release a wing from the acetate and insert a tiny amount of it into the freshly piped body. Place a tiny piece of sponge under the wing to support it while it dries, creating a lifelike pose. Repeat for the other wing. You can insert two stamen cottons into the head of the butterfly to create antennae. Stamen cottons are non-edible and must be removed before the cake is cut. Make two butterflies and attach one to the top of the cake and one to the lower cake drum.

*Details from the finished cake.*

# INDIAN INLAID CAKE

This beautiful cake has the look of sari fabric and is created using an inlaid design. It is important to use space bars when rolling out the fondant (sugarpaste) to cover the cake, so that the main covering and inlaid pieces are the same depth. You will also learn how to pipe with fondant (sugarpaste). Marzipan the cake and allow it to skin over before covering with fondant (sugarpaste).

**You will need**

17.5cm (7in) round cake, 7.5cm (3in) deep

25cm (10in) cake drum

650g (1lb 6oz) pink fondant (sugarpaste)

90g (3oz) pale jade fondant (sugarpaste)

90g (3oz) jade fondant (sugarpaste)

90g (3oz) green fondant (sugarpaste)

240g (½lb) royal icing

Edible liquid food colour (droplet) in old gold

Simple leaf cutters

Primrose cutter. 2.5cm (1in) diameter

Vodka

Scriber

Plastic side scraper

Palette knife

13mm (½in) round cutter

Piping bags size 1 and 2

Piping nozzles No.s 1, 1.5 and 2

Optional: FMM embosser (scroll set 1) for the iced cake drum

15mm (½in) satin ribbon

Non-toxic glue stick

Cash register receipt roll

Masking tape

1 Take a strip of cash register receipt roll the same length as the circumference of the cake plus an extra 13mm (½in). Fold it into six equal sections (do not incorporate the extra bit). Draw then cut a scallop in the folded strip.

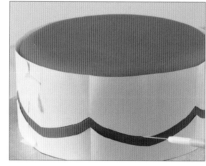

2 Unfold the length of paper and wrap both pieces round the cake leaving a 6mm (¼in) gap between the two strips. Secure the ends together with masking tape. Scribe the scallop design onto the cake. Remove the paper templates.

3 Find the central point of the curve in the scalloped design. Use the primrose cutter to cut and remove the piece of fondant (sugarpaste) from the cake covering.

4 Roll out a piece of pale jade fondant (sugarpaste) using space bars, and cut out six primrose flowers. Lightly moisten with vodka the marzipan that is now visible inside the cut-out, insert the pale jade primrose and lightly smooth the surface. Repeat to inlay all six flowers.

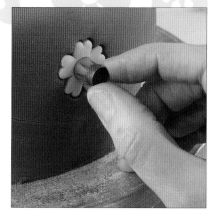

5 Roll out a piece of jade fondant (sugarpaste) using the space bars. Use the small round cutter to cut out six discs. Use the same cutter to remove the centres from the primrose flowers and inlay the jade discs.

6 Repeat this process for the leaves and teardrop shapes.

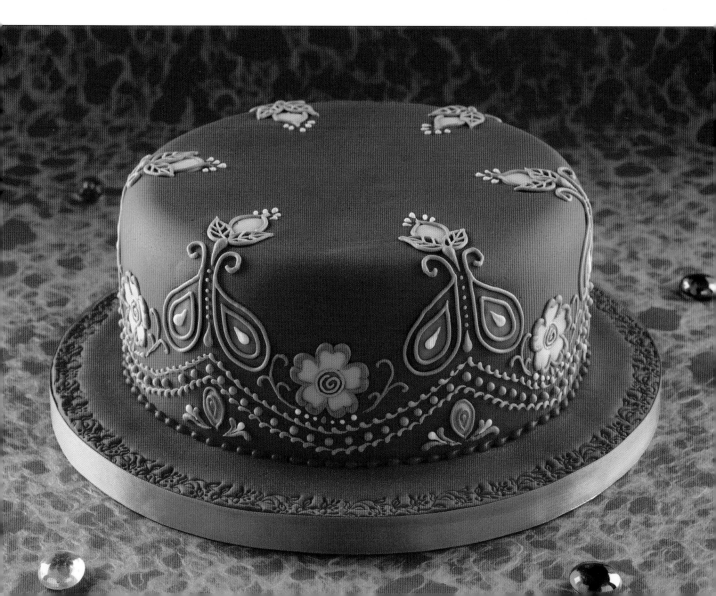

7 Cut small bud shapes from the top of the cake and inlay pale jade, with a green leaf on either side. Make sure you inlay one leaf before cutting the second out of the cake covering. Once the inlay is complete, cover the cake drum with fondant (sugarpaste) and emboss the edges. Leave the icing to skin over for twenty-four hours.

8 Tilt the cake. Overpipe the scribed scallop lines with a curved teardrop shape in old-gold-coloured royal icing, with a No. 1.5 nozzle.

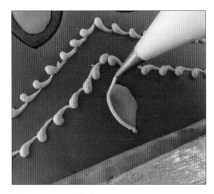

9 Pipe around the base teardrop inlays with a No. 1 nozzle and the same coloured royal icing.

10 Pressure pipe around the edge of the primroses with a No. 1.5 nozzle and the same coloured royal icing. Use a No. 1 nozzle and the same colour to outline the central disc.

11 Pipe a spiral on the central disc of each primrose with a No. 1 nozzle.

### Pressure piping

By applying a steady pressure to the filled piping bag, holding it in the same place at a 90 degree angle to the surface of the icing, you can make a piped dot fatten, giving the illusion that it was created using a larger piping nozzle.

Likewise by applying a steady pressure to the filled bag while the nozzle is dragged slowly over the surface of the icing at a 35 degree angle, it can appear that it was created with a larger nozzle.

By combining these two techniques, altering the angle to 35 degrees instead of 90, you can create a teardrop with a pointed end. If the final piping action causes the piped line to snap, move the piping bag faster in relation to the amount of pressure you apply.

12 Pipe a row of evenly spaced dots between the two rows of curved teardrops with a No. 1.5 nozzle. Pipe two dots, one at the point of each scallop, then add one in the centre between them, and continue subdividing until you have a full, even decoration of dots.

13 Outline each large leaf with No. 1.5 nozzle in a spiral design as shown, and each inner leaf with a No. 1 nozzle.

14 Outline each bud with a No. 1.5 nozzle as shown, then pipe the veins in the leaves using a No. 1 nozzle.

15 Outline the leaves with the No 1.5 nozzle.

16 Pipe two gold teardrops using a No. 1.5 nozzle: one coming down between the large green leaves and one in the opposite direction between the top twirls.

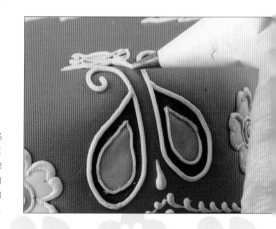

**17** Pipe five evenly spaced gold dots between the two large leaves with the No. 1 nozzle. Begin with the two end ones, pipe one centrally in between, then further subdivide with one more in each gap.

**18** Pipe a small gold teardrop centrally beneath each inlaid primrose with a No. 1 nozzle. Pipe three white dots, graduating in size, on either side of the gold teardrop, using a No. 1 nozzle.

**19** Pipe a white teardrop in the centre of each of the large inlaid leaves using the No 1. nozzle. Pipe a further small white teardrop at a 45 degree angle either side of the small inlaid teardrops around the base of the cake, using the same nozzle.

**20** Pipe five small white teardrops around the inlaid bud on the top edge of the cake with a No. 1 nozzle.

**21** Pipe two gold teardrops either side of the small white teardrops around the base of the cake, using a No. 1 nozzle.

**22** Pipe three alternating gold 'C's either side of the inlaid primroses, using a No. 1 nozzle.

$23$ Take a walnut-sized piece of pink fondant (sugarpaste) and dip it into a glass of water. Knead it, dip it again, then knead it a second time.

$24$ Transfer the piece of fondant (sugarpaste) to a plastic side scraper and continue to add water with a palette knife.

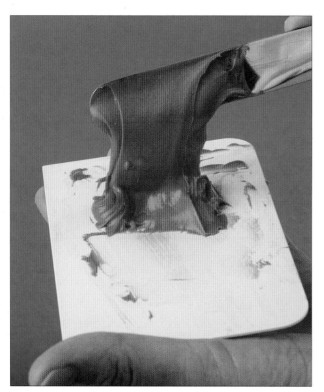

$25$ Paddle the fondant (sugarpaste) each time you add more water. Once the let-down fondant (sugarpaste) is soft enough to pipe with, use it to fill a size 2 piping bag with a No. 2 nozzle.

$26$ Pipe a snail's trail around the base of the cake with the let-down pink fondant (sugarpaste). Finish the cake by attaching a 15mm (½in) satin ribbon to the edge of the cake drum using a non-toxic glue stick..

*Details of the finished cake.*

# POPPY FIELD

In making this gorgeous poppy-themed cake, you will learn how to emboss a design from a piped template, create beautiful raised effects with brush embroidery and transfer an inscription using a pricking technique.

## You will need

15cm (6in) round cake, 10cm (4in) deep

22.5cm (9in) round cake drum

600g (20oz) marzipan

600g (20oz) fondant (sugarpaste)

240g (8oz) white royal icing

Small amount of white vegetable fat

Edible liquid food colours (droplet) in buttercup, fern green, holly green and old gold

Pure powder food colours in red and black

Piping nozzles: No. 0 (x 2), No. 1 (x 2) and No. 2 (x 3)

Piping bags size 1 and 2 and knee high (pop sock)

Sable paintbrush No. 2

Artist's palette knife

Scriber

Piece of sponge foam

Vodka

Turntable

Cake tilter

Food-grade acetate (butcher's wrap)

Sheet of perspex (plexiglass) approx. 35cm (14in) square

2 shot glasses and 2 pipettes

White edible shimmer petal dust

Masking tape

15mm (½in) double satin ribbon

Non-toxic glue stick

1 Secure the floral design (see page 124) to the underside of a piece of persex (plexiglass) with masking tape. Ensure that the stems and leaves part is level with the edge. Half fill a size 1 piping bag (No. 1 nozzle) with white royal icing. Pipe the design onto the perspex. Leave the piped design to dry for no less than thirty minutes.

2 As soon as the cake is covered with fondant (sugarpaste), hold the perspex (plexiglass) with the piped design against the side of the cake and press it firmly to emboss into the fondant (sugarpaste). Carefully rock the perspex onto the top of the cake and press firmly. Lift off. The piped design should still be on the perspex, but if any bits have broken off and are embedded in the covering icing, flick these off with a scriber.

**Tip**
You can keep the perspex (plexiglass) with the piped design on it and resuse it for other cakes. If you want to remove it, wash it off with cold water.

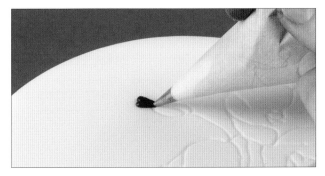

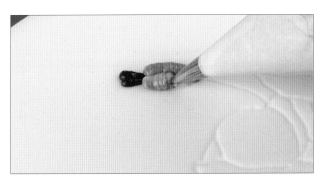

3 Place a tiny amount of red powder food colour in a shot glass and add a couple of drops of cooled boiled water to colour some royal icing. Half fill a size 2 piping bag (No. 2 nozzle) with red royal icing. Start piping at the top of the design and pressure pipe the two red petals (fat teardrop shapes) for the poppy bud. These need to conceal the embossed design.

4 Half fill a size 2 piping bag (No. 2 nozzle) with green royal icing (use equal quantities of fern and holly food colour). Pipe two fat teardrop shapes to create the sheath on the bud. Pipe the stem of this bud.

**Tip**

In brush embroidery, always start with the part of the design that is furthest away.

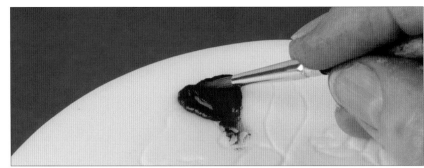

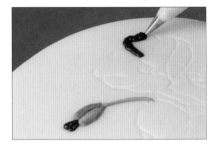

6 Dip the paintbrush in water and then remove the surplus with your index finger and thumbnail to flatten the bristles. Brush the red royal icing, starting at the central point of the edge of the petal, then fan out the brush strokes from the outside edge to the flower centre. The brush movement must stop at the flower centre and not before – even if you think there is no royal icing on the brush – to create a shaded petal rather than a flat petal with a raised outline. Outline one petal at a time and then brush it before outlining the next, or the royal icing will have dried before you can brush it. If the brush is too dry, it will pull the royal icing off the surface, but if it is too wet, there will be no brush stokes visible on the petals.

5 Starting with the furthest (background) petal, pressure pipe a fat red line around it with a No. 2 nozzle (see page 74).

7 Pressure pipe the outline of the petal to the right of the first one (the next one forwards, which should overlap). Brush the outline as before. Now repeat this process with the petal to the left of the first petal.

8 Place a tiny amount of black powder food colour in a shot glass and add a couple of drops of cooled boiled water to create the liquid food colour for the royal icing. Half fill a size 1 piping bag with a No. 0 nozzle with black royal icing. Pipe filament lines and dots for anthers.

9 Pipe the centre of the poppy (pistil) with green royal icing and a No. 2 nozzle. Correct the shape with a damp paintbrush. Leave to dry for a few minutes before piping more filaments and anthers on top.

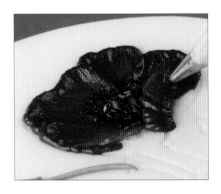

10 Pressure pipe the curled over petal, with red royal icing and a No. 2 nozzle, giving it plenty of depth.

11 Brush the piped shape from the petal edge to the base to create texture and smooth out certain areas if necessary.

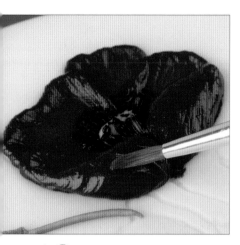

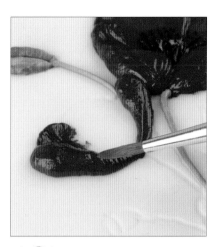

12 Pressure pipe the last petal on the flower. Brush the piped shape as before. Pipe the stem with green royal icing and a No. 2 nozzle.

13 Start piping the next poppy: brush the first petal and then pressure pipe the next two. Ensure that the two pressure-piped petals reduce in height as they get closer to the base of the flower. Pipe the stem as for the first poppy.

14 Pressure pipe the final, closest petal and make sure it slopes down at the base. Pipe the seed head and black stamens with a No. 0 nozzle, and a green pistil piped with a No. 2 nozzle.

15 Start piping the buttercups. Half fill a size 2 piping bag (No. 2 nozzle) with buttercup royal icing. Following the embossed design, pipe two fat teardrops to create the buds. Half fill a size 1 piping bag (No. 1 nozzle) with fern green royal icing and pipe the stems.

16 Pipe and brush the petals of the buttercups which are furthest away.

**17** Half fill a size 1 piping bag (No. 0 nozzle) with old gold royal icing and pipe the stamens on the buttercups.

**18** Pressure pipe the remaining petals on the buttercups with the size 2 piping bag and No. 2 nozzle filled in step 15. Pipe the calyxes on the buds.

**19** Pipe the stems and bracts on the buttercups. Continue working down the embossed design.

**20** As the poppy leaves are very large, it is easier to pipe and brush them in sections. Outline the leaf and brush from the outside edge towards the centre with the brushstrokes at a 45 degree angle.

**21** On completion of that section of the leaf, re-shape the brush to a point and then pull it up the centre of the leaf to create a midrib.

**22** Create the next poppy just as before.

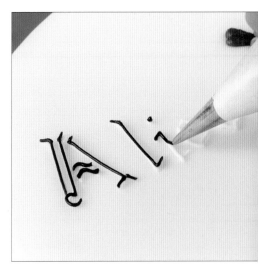

23 Write the inscription on a piece of paper. Place this on a piece of sponge foam and using the scriber, make a pin prick at each point where a line starts or changes direction. Place the piece of paper on top of the cake, sterilise the scriber with alcohol and re-pin prick the same points on the cake surface. Half fill a size 2 piping bag (No. 1 nozzle) with white royal icing. Using the dots as a guide, pipe the inscription.

24 Overpipe the inscription in black royal icing with a No. 0 nozzle.

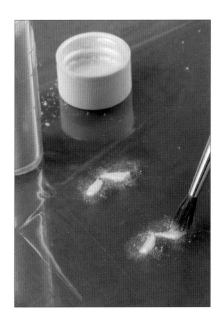

25 Place the bee template (see page 124) on a piece of perspex (plexiglass), cover with a piece of food grade acetate and secure with masking tape. Apply a tiny amount of white vegetable fat to the acetate, wipe off with kitchen paper. Take clean kitchen paper and wipe again. Pipe a small dot of white royal icing (No. 1 nozzle) at the broadest part of the wings, then use a damp paintbrush to brush the royal icing to the base point of the wings. The piped wings are very fragile, so pipe spares. Leave to dry no less than thirty minutes.

26 Dry dust the dried wings with a white edible shimmer petal dust.

27 Using a No. 2 piping nozzle with yellow royal icing, pipe a teardrop for the base of the body the same size as the template.

28 Overpipe part of the body using a No. 1 nozzle with black royal icing. Pipe the upper body. Use a damp paintbrush to create a fur-like texture.

29 Release the wings from the acetate by sliding an artist's palette knife underneath them. While the black icing is still fresh, insert the wings into the upper body. Leave to dry for no less than thirty minutes.

30 Once the bee has dried, release it from the acetate and secure it to the cake surface with a small amount of white royal icing. To finish the cake, attach a 15mm (½in) satin ribbon to the edge of the cake drum using a non-toxic glue stick.

**Opposite**
*A detail from the finished cake.*

# SCROLLS AND ROSES

This lavishly decorated cake would be perfect for an important wedding anniversary. You will learn how to create a gorgeous effect with scrolls and how to pipe intricate graduated linework. Make the piped roses using yellow royal icing and a No. 57 nozzle (see pages 44–45). It is optional to catch the edges of the dried roses with burgundy petal dust. Coat the cake and cake drum with royal icing (see pages 26–30).

## You will need

15cm (6in) round cake, 10cm (4in) deep

22.5cm (9in) cake drum

Piping nozzles No.s 1, 2, 3, 43, 44 and 57

Piping bags size 1, 2, 3, and 4

Scissors

Scriber

Cake tilter

Scalpel and cutting mat or sticky notes

Sable paintbrush No. 2

Edible liquid food colours (droplet) in buttercup and fern green

Burgundy edible petal dust

900g (2lb) white royal icing

13mm (½in) double satin ribbon

Non-toxic glue stick

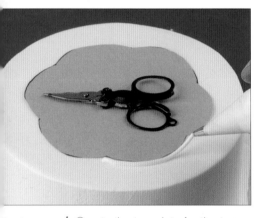

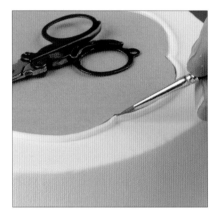

1 Create the template for the top of the cake from the design on page 125. Place it centrally with a small weighted item on top to hold it in place. Half fill a size 3 piping bag (No. 3 nozzle) with white royal icing. Pipe a line as close to the template as possible without touching. Stop and restart the line at every point.

2 Use a damp paintbrush if necessary to tidy or sharpen the joins.

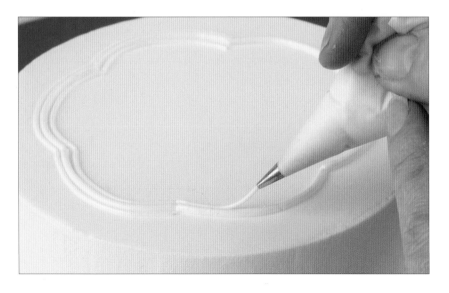

3 Carefully remove the template. Half fill a size 2 piping bag (No. 2 nozzle) with white royal icing. Pipe a line either side of the first line. These lines need to be as close as possible without touching. Stop and restart the line at every point. Use a damp paintbrush as before to tidy or sharpen the joins.

**4** Using the same piping bag and nozzle, pipe a line directly on top of the first line (the one you did with the No. 3 nozzle). Use a damp paintbrush if necessary.

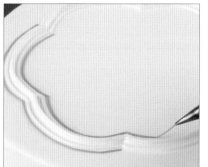

**5** Half fill a size 2 piping bag (No. 1 nozzle) with green royal icing. Pipe a green line either side of the outer white No. 2 nozzle lines. Make sure the green lines are as close as possible without touching. Stop and restart the line at every point and use a paintbrush as before if needed.

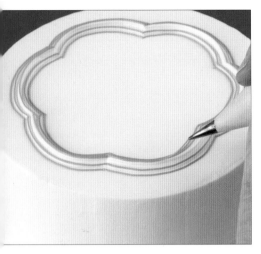

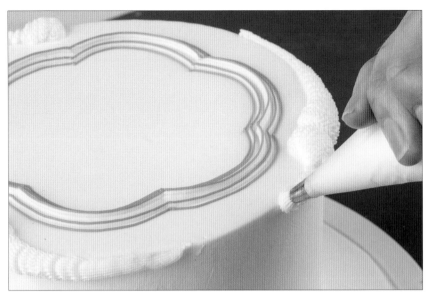

6 Overpipe the other piped white lines with the green royal icing.

7 Divide the top edge of the cake into six sections with a dot of royal icing, using the No. 2 nozzle. These sections should line up with points on the piped design.Half fill a size 4 piping bag (No. 44 nozzle) with white royal icing. You can pipe agitated or rope scrolls, but be consistent throughout the cake. Those shown are agitated scrolls. The scroll needs to start on the top of the cake (at the dot), move down on to the cake side, then finish on the top at the next dot. The scrolls on this cake are alternating (mirror image): the first scrolls starts from the left and goes anticlockwise (to the right), and the next scroll starts on the right and goes clockwise (to the left).

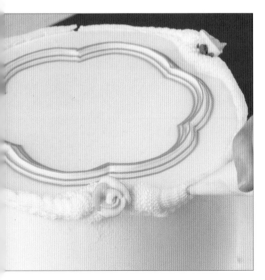

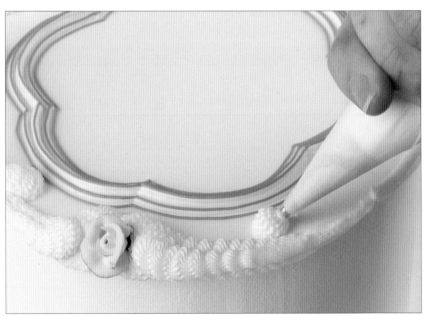

8 Position three piped roses on the top edge of the cake while the royal icing is still soft. Half fill a size 4 piping bag (No. 43 nozzle) with white royal icing. Overpipe the alternating scrolls.

9 Pipe another set of alternating scrolls (No. 43 nozzle) on the top of the cake: start at the centre of a scallop's curve and finish at the same point as the first set of alternating scrolls.

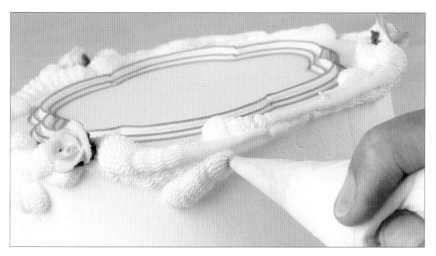

10 Pipe another set of alternating scrolls on the side of the cake, starting halfway between the first and second scroll and finishing at the same point as the first set of alternating scrolls.

11 Divide the base of the cake into six sections with a dot of royal icing (No. 2 nozzle). These sections should line up with the previous dots. Pipe alternating scrolls between the dots, with a No.44 nozzle.

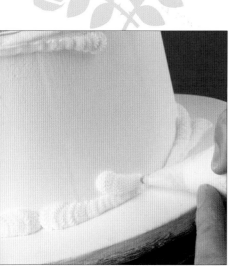

12 Pipe the additional alternating scrolls along the base with the No. 43 nozzle.

13 Attach the piped roses along the base while the royal icing is still soft.

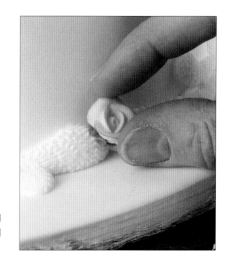

14 Pipe a group of five teardrops (No 3 nozzle) on the top of the cake. Pipe another group of teardrops on the side of the cake (at the base of the roses along the top edge).

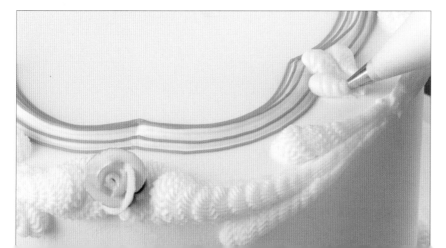

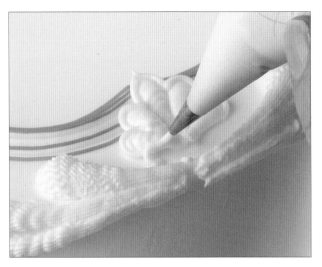

**15** Outline these teardrops with a No. 2 nozzle, finishing with two alternating 'C's.

**16** Overpipe the No. 2 white line with green royal icing, using the No. 1 nozzle.

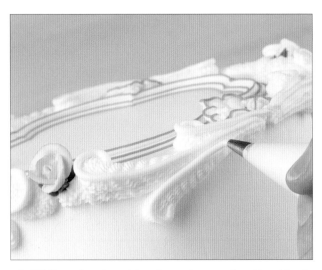

**17** Overpipe the white alternating scrolls with a No. 3 nozzle and white royal icing.

**18** Overpipe the No. 3 lines in white with a No. 2 nozzle.

**19** Overpipe the No 2. white lines with green royal icing using a No. 1 nozzle.

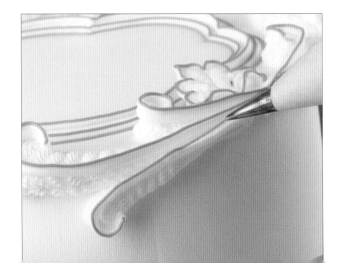

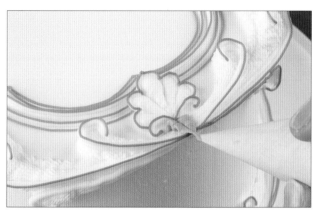

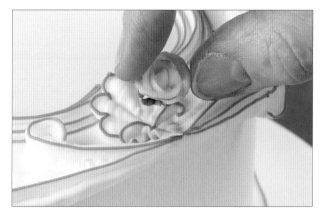

20 Create a piping bag for piping leaves (see page 45). Half fill with green royal icing. Pipe a leaf at the base of each group of No. 3 teardrops on the top of the cake.

21 Attach the piped roses while the royal icing is still soft.

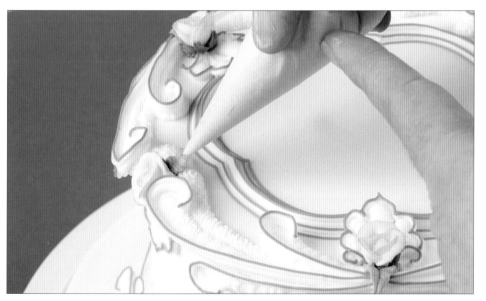

22 Pipe another leaf at the back of each rose.

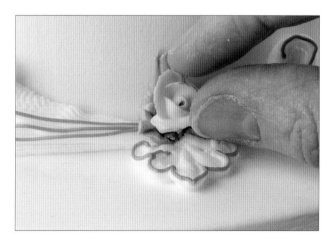

23 Pipe three leaves around the other roses along the top edge.

24 Pipe a group of three leaves, then attach a rose where each group of teardrops at the base of the cake is piped.

25 Copy the template on page 125. Place it on a cutting mat or a block of sticky notes and carefully cut along the lines using a scalpel. Secure the template to the side of the cake with a few dots of royal icing. Carefully scribe the design onto the side of the cake.

26 Tilt the cake and overpipe the scribed lines with a No. 2 nozzle and white royal icing. Pipe a group of three teardrops centrally at the base of the design. Overpipe the teardrops with a No. 2 nozzle.

27 Pipe three green dots (No. 2 nozzle) graduating in size at the centre of the design. Pipe two alternating teardrops at either side of the design. Overpipe the No. 2 lines in green royal icing with a No. 1 nozzle.

28 Half fill a size 2 piping bag (No. 2 nozzle) with buttercup royal icing and pipe the final group of dots and a teardrop below as shown. To finish the cake, attach a 13mm (½in) satin ribbon to the edge of the cake drum with non-toxic glue stick, overlapping at the back of the cake by 13mm (½in).

94

*Details from the finished cake. Once the piped roses are fully dry, dry dust with burgundy edible petal dust.*

# EDWARDIAN STYLE

This beautiful deep cake is topped with spectacular royal icing frills. It has an unusual colour scheme and would suit an autumn wedding or birthday. You will learn how to pipe in two-tone royal icing. Create the piped roses with marigold royal icing and the No. 57 nozzle (see pages 44–45). Marzipan the cake. Prepare the chamfered cake drum (see page 33). Coat the cake (see pages 28–29) and cake drum with white royal icing.

1 Make a paper template the same size as the top of the cake and divide it into nine equal 40 degree sections. Mark and cut away a concave scallop shape in each section.For the side template, wrap a piece of paper round the cake and divide the length into nine equal sections. Draw and cut a convex scallop at one end of each section and a concave scallop at the other. Place the top template centrally on the cake and place a small weighted item on top to hold it in place. Wrap the side template round the cake, securing it with a piece of masking tape. Make sure the points on both templates are aligned. Half fill a size 1 piping bag (No. 1 nozzle) with white royal icing. Pipe a line as close to the template as possible without touching. Stop and restart the line at every point.

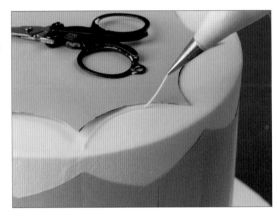

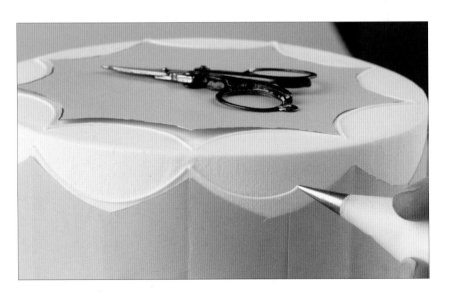

2 Using the same piping bag, pipe a line as close to the top edge of the side template as possible without touching. Stop and restart the line at every point.

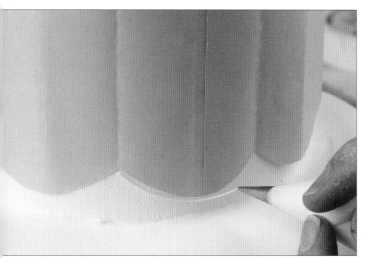

3 Using the same piping bag, pipe a line round the base of the side template in the same way. Carefully remove the template.

4 Half fill a size 4 piping bag (No. 44 nozzle) with white royal icing. Pipe an 'S' scroll directly on top of the No. 1 piped line. This can be in the agitated or rope style but keep it consistent throughout the cake (the ones shown are agitated). Start on the top of the cake at the point of a scallop, follow the line along the top of the cake until you reach the next point and then continue piping the scroll onto the side of the cake following the scallop line there. Finish the scroll on the edge of cake at the next point.

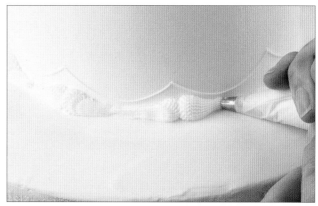

5 Complete the 'S' scrolls at the top of the cake as shown.

6 Pipe alternating scrolls around the base of the cake as shown.

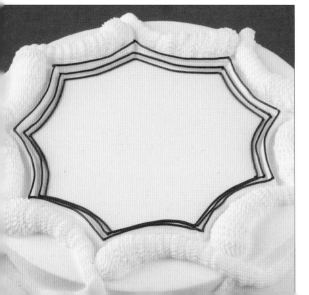

7 Half fill a size 3 piping bag with (No. 3 nozzle) with white royal icing. Half fill a size 2 piping bag (No 2 nozzle) with white royal icing. Half fill a size 1 piping bag (No. 1 nozzle) with brown royal icing. Pipe graduated linework on the top of the cake following the scalloped shape of the scrolls. Start with a No. 3 nozzle and stop and restart the line at every point. Use a damp paintbrush if necessary to tidy or sharpen the joins. Pipe a No. 2 white line in the same way, as close as possible to the No 3 line without touching. Now pipe a No. 2 line directly on top of the No. 3 line. Pipe a No. 1 brown line as close as possible to the No. 2 line, without touching. Pipe a brown No. 1 line on top of the No. 2 line and then directly on top the line which is made up of a No. 3 and No. 2 line.

8 Create a size 4 piping bag (No. 57 nozzle) for two-tone royal icing. Half fill a No. 2 piping bag (without a nozzle) with marigold royal icing and half fill a size 3 piping bag (with no nozzle) with white royal icing. Cut the end point off the marigold-filled piping bag and squeeze this icing down the side of the No.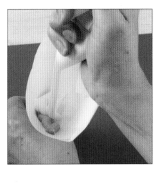
4 piping bag, making sure it is on the side where the No. 57 nozzle is the thinnest. Cut the end off the other piping bag and squeeze this icing down the other side of the piping bag. Fold the No. 4 piping bag down in the normal way. Squeeze a small amount out to check that both colours are visible. The proportion of colour can be altered slightly by carefully turning the nozzle in the piping bag.

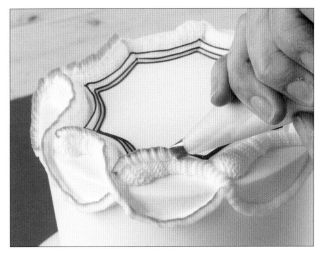

9 Using this piping bag, pipe directly on top of the 'S' scrolls on the cake top to make the frills. Ensure that the broad end of No. 57 nozzle is touching the scroll as you pipe.

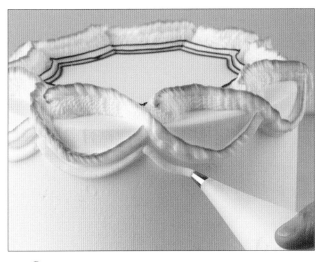

10 Half fill a size 3 piping bag (No. 42 nozzle) with white royal icing. Pipe a dropped loop underneath the 'S' scrolls, as close as possible without touching.

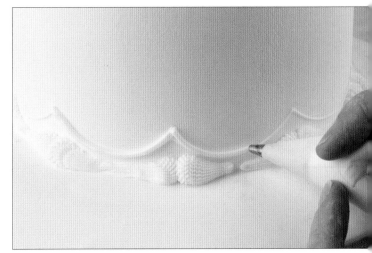

11 Pipe a dropped loop around the base of the cake, following the line piped in step 3, using the No. 3 piping nozzle.

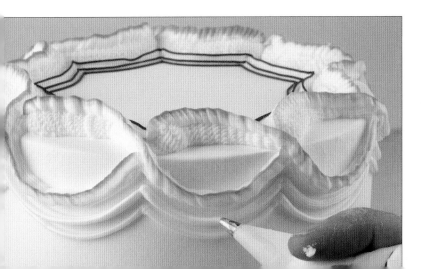

12 Using the No. 3 piping nozzle, pipe a dropped loop under the No 42 loops (as close as possible without touching). Using the same nozzle, overpipe the No 42 loops.

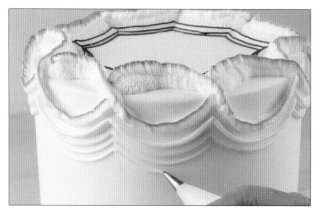

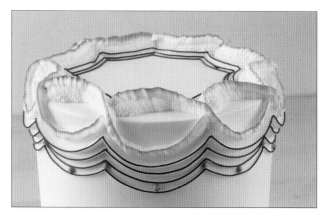

**13** Using the No. 2 nozzle, pipe a dropped loop under the No. 3 loops, as close as possible without touching. Using the same nozzle, overpipe the No. 3 and No. 42 loops. Pipe a further row of No. 2 loops approx. 5mm (¼in) lower than the previous loops.

**14** Overpipe all of the loops with brown royal icing and a No. 1 nozzle. Half fill a size 2 piping bag (No. 2 nozzle) with marigold royal icing which has been let down slightly with a couple of drops of water. Pipe bulbs between the two rows of dropped loops. The easiest way to keep the bulbs even is to start by piping bulbs at each point and the central point of the loops. Then keep subdividing the space between two bulbs.

**15** Complete the piped loops around the base of the cake with a No. 2 nozzle and white royal icing: pipe two rows of loops above the No. 3 loops and then one row on top of the No. 3 loops.

**16** Overpipe the scrolls round the base of the cake with alternating 'C's using the No. 3 nozzle. Overpipe this shape with white royal icing and a No. 2 nozzle.

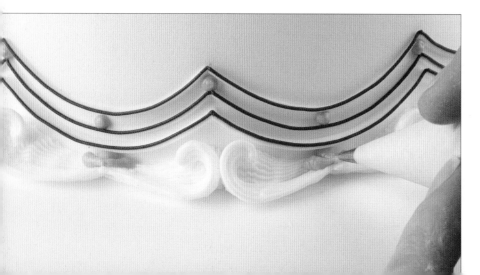

**17** Overpipe the loops round the base of the cake with brown royal icing and a No. 1 nozzle. Pipe evenly spaced bulbs (see step 15) between the two top rows of loops around the base. Pipe a group of three teardrop shapes above the central point of the alternating scrolls.

18 Tilt the cake and pipe two alternating white 'C's with a No. 2 nozzle on the side of the cake to create a heart shape.

19 Repeat this process and create a small heart at the central point of the first heart. Overpipe the heart shapes with brown royal icing, using a No. 1 nozzle.

20 Overpipe the base scrolls with brown royal icing, using the No. 1 nozzle.

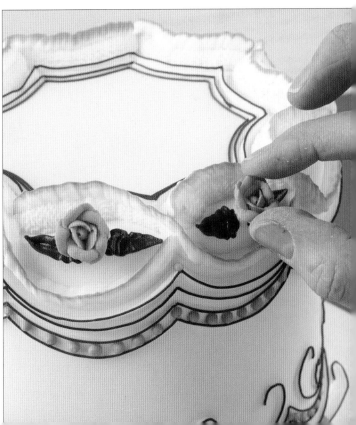

21 Create a size 3 piping bag for piping leaves (see page 45) Half fill the piping bag with brown royal icing. Use to pipe the leaves around the top edge of the cake. Attach the piped roses.

22 Pipe a group of three leaves where shown and attach a rose on top of each group round the base of the cake.

23 Using the No. 2 nozzle and white royal icing, pipe loops around the base edge of the cake drum.

24 Pipe a row of loops above the No. 2 loops, as close as possible without touching, using a No. 1 nozzle and brown royal icing. Repeat below the No. 2 loops. Complete the graduated linework by piping a row of loops directly on top of the No. 2 loops. Pipe a group of three small teardrops at the point of each scallop. To finish the cake, attach a 13mm (½in) satin ribbon to the edge of the cake drum using a non-toxic glue stick. Overlap the ribbon at the back of the cake by 13mm (½in).

*Details of the finished cake.*

# MODERN BLACKWORK

This striking cake was inspired by floral tattoos and henna designs, as well as by blackwork embroidery. It features freehand piping, using a template and brush embroidery. You will also learn how to create a beautiful butterfly on acetate and transfer it to the cake top. Cover the cake with marzipan and fondant (sugarpaste) and ideally leave it to skin over before commencing any decoration.

## You will need

15cm (6in) round cake, 7.5cm (3in) deep

22.5cm (9in) cake drum

Piping nozzles No.s 0, 1 and 2

Piping bags size 1 and 2 and knee high (pop sock)

240g (8oz) of royal icing

Pure powdered food colour in black and red

2 shot glasses and 2 pipettes

Cake tilter

Edible liquid food colours (droplet) in yellow and orange

Edible petal dusts in green, red, orange and yellow

Vodka

Sable paintbrush, No. 2

Scriber

Tweezers

Artist's palette knife

Sheet of perspex (plexiglass)

Kitchen paper

Food-grade acetate (butcher's wrap)

White vegetable fat

Masking tape

Small amount of sponge foam

15mm (½in) double-sided satin ribbon

Non-toxic glue stick

Black stamen cottons (optional)

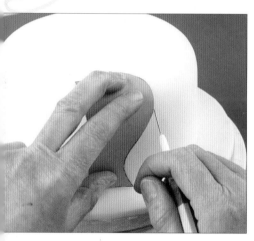

1 Divide the side of the covered cake into six equal sections. Using template A (page 126), scribe a curved line in each section. Stop the scribed line 15mm (½in) above the base of the cake.

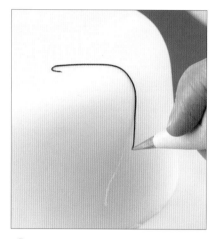

2 Half fill a size 1 piping bag (No. 1 nozzle) with black royal icing, made from the powdered food colour as in step 3, page 81. Place the cake on a tilter and pipe the scribed line, which will be a stem.

3 Freehand pipe the branches from the stem.

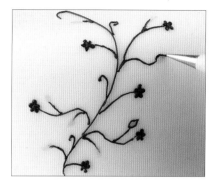

4 Using the same piping bag and nozzle, pipe five teardrops to make flowers. Mix green petal dust with a tiny amount of alcohol to create a paint. Use a fine paintbrush to paint leaves on the ends of the piped branches, freehand.

5 Once the leaves are dry, pipe an outline around them with the black royal icing and the No. 1 nozzle.

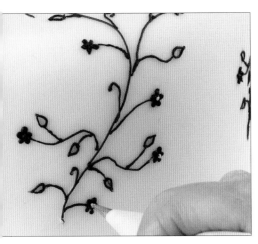

6 Half fill a size 1 piping bag (No. 1 nozzle) with yellow royal icing and pipe the centres of the small teardrop flowers. The black royal icing must be completely dry, otherwise there is a risk of the black colouring bleeding into the yellow.

7 Using a paper template made from the flower design on page 126, scribe the primrose at the base of each piped stem. Half should be on the side of the cake and the remaining half on the covered cake drum.

8 Use the various leaf templates (see page 126) to scribe leaf shapes around the primrose flowers.

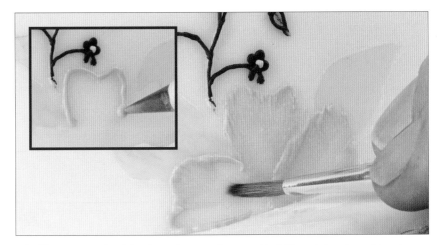

9 Paint the leaves with a mixture of green petal dust and alcohol. Scribe the next set of primrose flowers and leaves around the edge of the covered cake drum, then paint the remaining leaves.

10 Brush embroider the primrose flowers. Half fill a piping bag (No. 1 nozzle) with yellow royal icing. Pipe the outline of one of the petals (inset). Dip a No. 2 sable paintbrush in water and then remove the surplus by flattening the bristles with your index finger and thumbnail. Brush the royal icing. Start at the central point of the edge of the petal and then fan the brush strokes from the outside edge to the flower centre. The brush movement must stop at the centre of the flower and not before – even if you think there is no royal icing on the brush. This will ensure a shaded petal is created and not a petal with a royal icing outline. Outline one petal at a time and then brush it before outlining the next, or the royal icing will have dried before you have a chance to brush it. If the brush is too dry, it will pull the royal icing off the surface of the cake, but if it is too wet, there will be no brush stokes visible on the petals.

11 Half fill a piping bag (No. 0 nozzle) with black royal icing. Scratch pipe a central line down each large leaf by dragging the nozzle in the cake surface as you pipe. Pipe the veins from the central line to the leaf edge. Re-pipe the central vein of the leaves. Pressure pipe the outline of the leaves using a No. 1 piping nozzle.

12 Pressure pipe the outline of the primrose flower with black royal icing and a No. 1 nozzle. Pipe the centres of the primrose flowers with black royal icing and a No. 0 nozzle.

13 Fill some of the open spaces around the primrose flowers with stretched teardrop shapes.

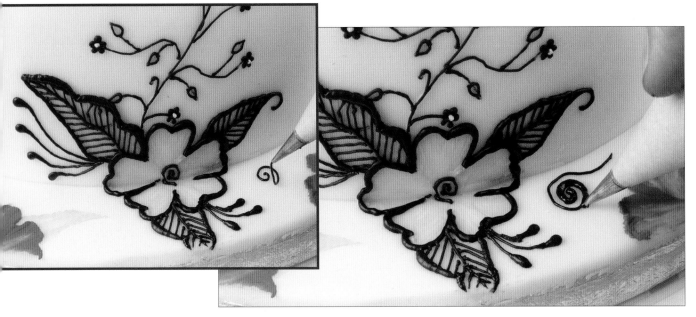

14 Fill some of the remaining open spaces with freehand piped spirals – these look more effective if they are pressure piped, but you might find it easier to pipe the spiral with a No. 0 nozzle first and then pressure pipe over this shape with a No. 1 nozzle.

15 Finish the primrose flowers by piping three tiny lines on each petal of the flower.

16 Secure a piece of food-grade acetate or wax paper to a sheet of perspex (plexiglass) or a flat board, with a few pieces of masking tape. Apply a tiny amount of white vegetable fat to the acetate and then wipe it off. Take a clean piece of kitchen paper and wipe the surface of the acetate again. If there is too much fat on the surface, it will break down the royal icing. Slide the butterfly template (see page 126) under the piece of acetate. Half fill a piping bag (No. 2 nozzle) with white royal icing. Pipe a small amount of royal icing at the base of each wing and then brush it, fanning out the brush strokes from the base of the wing. Create the same shape as the outline on the template. Complete all four wings.

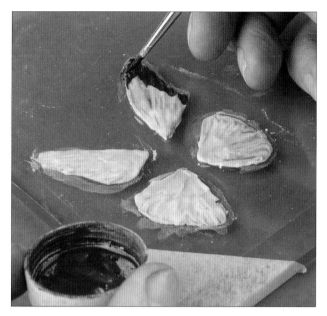

17 Once the wings are dry, paint them with petal dust mixed with alcohol. I have used yellow close to the body, radiating out to orange and then red at the tips.

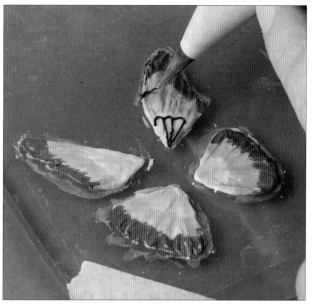

18 Pipe the details on the wings with black royal icing and the No. 0 piping nozzle.

19 Complete all the wings.

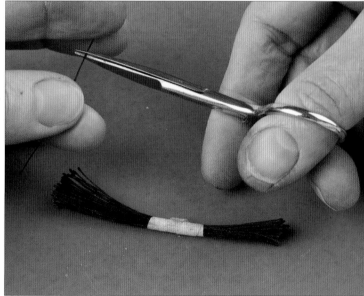

20 Creating the antennae of the butterflies is optional. If you opt to use the stamen cottons, then this item needs to be classed as non-edible and must be removed before the cake is cut. Cut a stamen cotton in half.

21 Pipe a body for the butterfly on top of the cake with black royal icing and a No. 2 nozzle. Use the artist's palette knife to release the butterfly wings from the acetate. Insert a tiny amount of each wing into the freshly piped body. Place a tiny piece of sponge foam under each wing to create a more lifelike pose.

22 If you are using them, insert two stamen cottons into the head of the butterfly to create the antennae. Once dry, the sponge supports can be removed. To finish the cake, attach a 15mm (½in) satin ribbon to the edge of the cake drum using a non-toxic glue stick.

*Details of the finished cake.*

# STEAMPUNK

In making this mouthwatering chocolate fondant (sugarpaste) cake, you will learn how to make run sugar decorations and pipe a convincing chain.

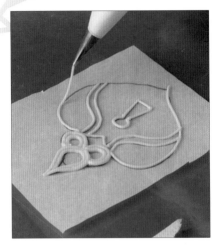

1 First make the run-outs (run sugar pieces). Secure a piece of food-grade acetate or wax paper to a piece of perspex (plexiglass) or a flat board, with a few pieces of masking tape. Apply a tiny amount of white vegetable fat to the acetate and then wipe it off with a piece of kitchen paper. Take another clean piece of kitchen paper and wipe again.

**Tip**
Too much white vegetable fat left on the surface will break down the royal icing.

2 Half fill two size 2 piping bags, one with a No. 2 nozzle and the other with a No.1.5 nozzle, with royal icing coloured gold. Slide the heart-shaped lock template (see page 127) under the acetate. Pipe the design onto the acetate: the top section with a No. 2 and the base section with the No. 1.5 nozzle. Remove the template from under the acetate. Create the run sugar: place a small amount of gold-coloured royal icing in a bowl and add a tiny amount of water, stirring with a knife. Continue to add water until the royal icing levels itself out in nine seconds (less than that amount of time means the run sugar is too thin, more and it is too thick). Cover the bowl of run sugar with a damp cloth and leave it to settle for thirty minutes.

**Tip**
Always make spare run sugar pieces in case of breakage.

## You will need

15cm (6in) hexagonal cake, 7.5cm (3in) deep
22.5cm (9in) cake drum
650g (22oz) chocolate fondant (sugarpaste)
Space bars
240g (8oz) maroon fondant (sugarpaste)
240g (8oz) royal icing
Edible liquid food colour (droplet) in old gold
Piping nozzles: No.s 1, 1.5 and 2
Piping bags size 1, 2 and 3
Veining/Dresden tool
Scriber
Artist's palette knife
Food-grade acetate
White vegetable fat
Masking tape
Clear edible spray varnish
Edible metallic spray in gold and bronze
Edible liquid metallic paint in gold
A few pieces of perspex (plexiglass) 5mm (¼in) thick
Anglepoise lamp
Food dehydrator
15mm (½in) satin ribbon
Non-toxic glue stick
Kitchen paper
Paintbrush
Bowl
Knife

3 Switch on the food dehydtator and the anglepoise lamp, to heat the bulb. Cut through the bubbles on the surface of the run sugar with a knife. Pour it into a size 3 piping bag to half fill it. Wind the piping bag down in the normal way to create a neat parcel.

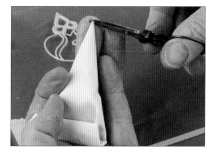

4 Snip the tip off the piping bag to make a hole no larger than a No. 1.5 nozzle. Flood the middle section of the heart lock. Use a paintbrush to pull the run sugar into all of the areas. Place the run-out under the anglepoise lamp to dry with the bulb approx. 15cm (6in) above it.

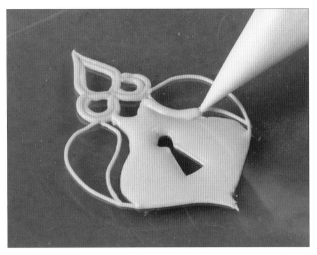

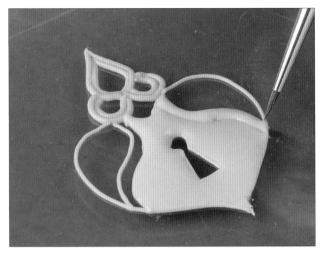

5 Once the run sugar has skinned over (approx. five minutes), flood the small strip either side of the middle (flooded) section.

6 Use a paintbrush to pull the run sugar into the points.

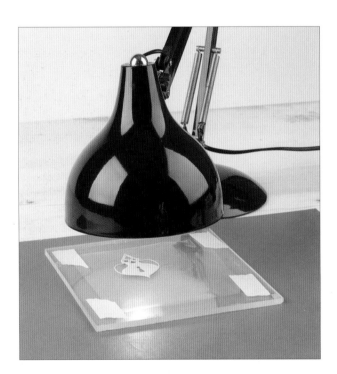

7 Place the run-out under the anglepoise lamp to dry as before.

8 Once the run sugar has skinned over, flood in the final two sections of the heart lock. Place the run-out under the anglepoise lamp, but this time leave it for twenty minutes.

9 Transfer the run-out to the food dehydrator to dry. All run-outs – no matter what their size – should be fully dry in twenty-four hours. Repeat this process with the other run-outs – cogs, key, and pointers (see the templates on page 127).

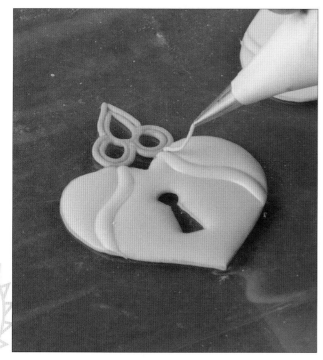

10 Once the run-outs are dry, half fill two size 1 piping bags (No. 0 and No. 1 nozzles) with standard consistency royal icing and then pipe on the embellishments.

11 Spray the heart lock and half of the cogs with edible metallic gold spray, and spray the remaining run-outs with the edible metallic bronze spray. Then spray all of them with the clear edible spray varnish to seal the metallic colour.

12 Cover the cake and cake drum with chocolate fondant (sugarpaste). Ideally, leave the it to skin over before continuing. Roll out a strip of maroon-coloured fondant (sugarpaste) using 3mm (1/8in) space bars. Moisten the base edge of the cake with water. Attach the strip of fondant starting at one of the corners, leaving at least 2.5cm (1in) overlap. Wrap the strip around the cake. Squeeze the two ends together and then use a pair of scissors to cut away the excess, creating a neat join.

13 Use the veining/Dresden tool to create a texture on the maroon strip, giving it the look of a ribbon.

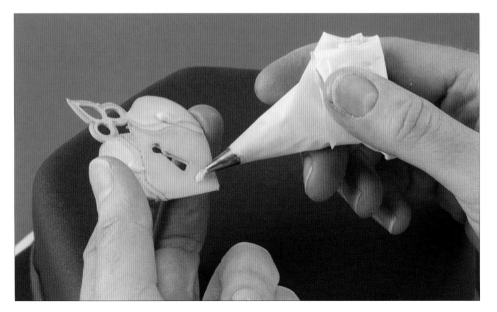

14 Release the heart lock run-out from the acetate by sliding the artist's palette knife beneath it. Take care not to bend the artist's palette knife while doing this, as that could cause the run-out to break. Pipe a few dots of royal icing on the back of the run-out and attach it to the cake top.

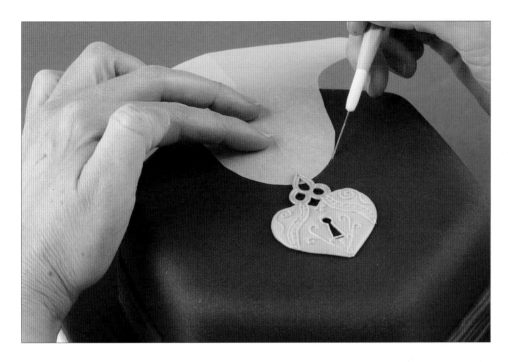

15 Carefully slide the template for the chain (see page 127) under the tip of the heart lock. Use a scriber to lightly scribe the outline for the chain on the cake surface.

16 Using a No. 1 piping nozzle and following the scribed line, pipe small oval shapes for the chain, leaving a small gap between each one.

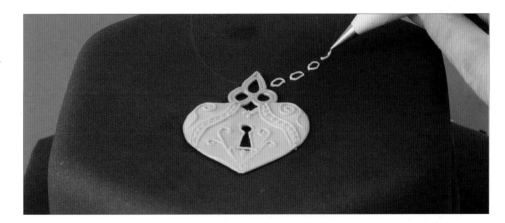

17 Pipe a loop between each oval and use a damp paintbrush to ensure that both ends of the loop touch the surface of the cake.

18 Paint the piped chain with edible liquid gold paint.

19 Attach the run sugar pointers to the cake side on two of the corners with a few dots of royal icing. Attach the run sugar key to the front corner in the same way.

20 Attach a group of cogs to the cake side on three of the corners. To finish the cake, attach a 15mm (½in) satin ribbon to the edge of the cake drum using a non-toxic glue stick.

*Details of the finished cake.*

# TEMPLATES FOR PIPING BASIC SHAPES

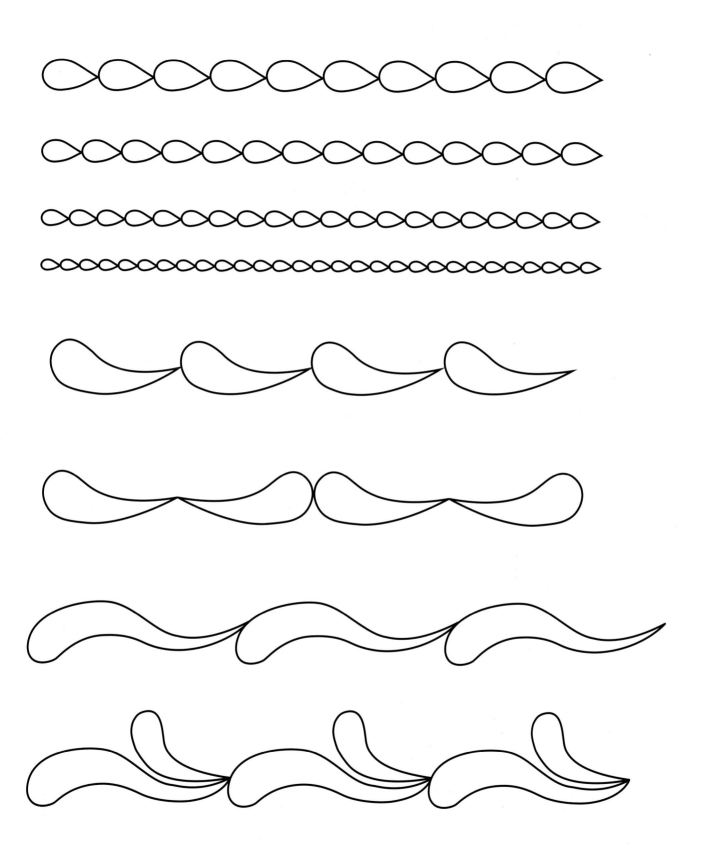

# CAKE DESIGN TEMPLATES

All templates are shown full size.

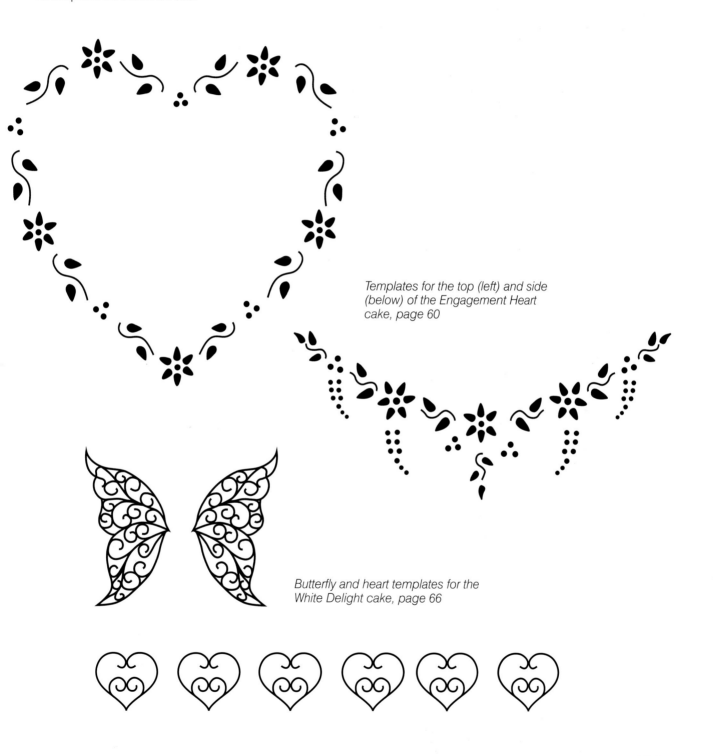

*Templates for the top (left) and side (below) of the Engagement Heart cake, page 60*

*Butterfly and heart templates for the White Delight cake, page 66*

*Templates for the piped embossed poppy design and the bee for the Poppy Field cake, page 80*

*Butterfly, primrose and leaf templates for the Modern Blackwork cake, page 104*

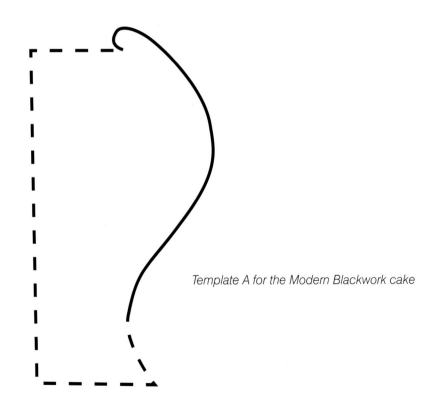

*Template A for the Modern Blackwork cake*

*Chain template for the Steampunk cake*

# INDEX